Copycat Appetizers Cookbook

Recipes From Your Favorite Restaurants

Copyright

Copyright 2019 New Wave Publishing. All rights reserved under International and Pan-American Copyright Conventions. No rights granted to reproduce this book or portions thereof in any form or manner whatsoever without the express written permission of the copyright owner(s).

Legal Notice

Content in this book is provided "As Is". The authors and publishers provide no guarantees regarding results of any advice or recommendations contained herein. Much of this book is based on personal experiences of the author(s) and anecdotal evidence. Although the author and publisher have made reasonable attempts to for accuracy in the content, they assume no responsibility for its veracity, or for any errors or omissions. Nothing in this book is intended to replace common sense, medical, legal or other professional advice. This book is meant only to be informative and entertaining. Encore Books and its authors shall not be liable in the event of incidental or consequential damages in connection with, or arising out of, the providing of the information offered herein.

Any trademarks, service marks, product names or named features are assumed to be the property of their respective owners and are used herein for reference purposes only. This book was not prepared, approved, licensed, or endorsed by any of the owners of the trademarks or brand names referred to in this book. There is no implied endorsement for any products or services mentioned in this publication.

Get Free Recipe eBooks!
Cookbook Club

Fabulous Free eBook Cookbooks Every Week!

Our eBooks are FREE for the first few days publication. Be the first to know when new books are published. Our collection includes hundreds of books on topics including healthy foods, diets, food allergy alternatives, gourmet meals, desserts, and easy and inexpensive meals.

Join the mailing list at:
EncoreBookClub.com

Related Copycat Books
Copycat Candy Recipes
http://url80.com/copycatcandy
Homemade Copycat Liqueurs
http://url80.com/copycatliqueur
Copycat Olive Garden Recipes
http://url80.com/copycatolive
Copycat PF Chang's Recipes
http://url80.com/copycatpfchang
Copycat Dessert Recipes
http://url80.com/copycatdessert
Copycat Applebee's Recipes
http://url80.com/copycatapplebee
Copycat Panera Bread Recipes
http://url80.com/copycatpanera
Copycat TGI Friday's Recipes
http://url80.com/fridays

Table of Contents

DIPS AND SAUCES — 1

California Pizza Kitchen Tuscan Hummus	2
Cheddar's Santa Fe Spinach Dip	4
Chevy's Mango Salsa	5
Carrabba's Bread Dipping Blend	6
Chili's Salsa	7
Cheesecake Factory Warm Crab & Artichoke Dip	8
Joe's Crab Shack Blue Crab Dip	10
Olive Garden Spinach-Artichoke Dip	11
Red Robin Campfire Sauce	12
Ruby Tuesday Queso Dip	12
Houston's Chicago Style Spinach Dip	13
Margaritaville Crab, Shrimp and Mushroom Dip	14
On the Border Guacamole Live	16
Olive Garden Hot Artichoke Spinach Dip	17

BREADS & BISCUITS — 18

Applebee's Pizza Sticks	19
Buca Di Beppo Garlic Bread	20
Little Caesar's Italian Bread Sticks	21
Cheesecake Factory Sweet Corn Tamale Cakes	22
Outback Steakhouse Honey Wheat Bushman	24
Popeyes Buttermilk Biscuits	25
Pizza Hut Cheese Bread	26
Red Lobster Cheddar Bay Biscuits	28

MORE APPETIZERS — 29

Abuelo Jalapeno Poppers	30
Applebee's Chicken Wings	31
Applebee's Baja Potato Boats	32
Applebee's Onion Peels with Dipping Sauce	34
Bahama Breeze West Indies Patties	36
Applebee's Chicken Quesadilla	39
Bar Louie Loaded Tots	40
Benigan's Chicken Quesadillas	41
Benihana Spicy Edamame	42

BJ's Restaurant Avocado Wraps	43
BJ's Restaurant Sriracha Brussels Sprouts	44
BJ's Restaurant Root Beer Glazed Ribs	45
Bonefish Grill Bang Bang Shrimp	46
Buca di Beppo World Famous Meatball	47
Buffalo Wild Wings Ultimate Nachos	48
Carraba's Italian Grill Zucchini Frittes	49
Cheddars Scratch Kitchen Texas Cheese Fries	50
Cheesecake Factory Tamale Cakes	51
Cheesecake Factory Mini Crab Cakes	52
Cheesecake Factory Avocado Eggrolls	54
Chili's Southwest Egg Rolls with Avocado Dipping Sauce	56
Chili's Boneless Shanghai Wings	58
Chili's Chicken Crispers	59
Chili's Chicken Fajita Nachos	60
Chili's Cheddar Cheese Bites	61
Chipotle Baba Ghanoush	62
Chipotle Guacamole	63
Claim Jumper Cheese Potato Cakes	64
Ikea Swedish Meatballs	66
Cracker Barrel Grilled Chicken Tenders	68
Joe's Crab Shack Great Balls of Fire	69
Joe's Crab Shack Crab Nacho's	70
KFC Honey BBQ Wings	71
Hooters Buffalo Wings	72
Houlihan's Shrooms	74
Hard Rock Cafe Tupelo Style Chicken	76
Hooter's Fried Pickles	77
Logan's Roadhouse Fried Mushrooms	78
Lone Star Steakhouse Amarillo Cheese Fries	79
Lavo's "The Meatball"	80
Longhorn Steakhouse Parmesan Encrusted Asparagus	82
Margaritaville Volcano Nachos	83
Longhorn Steakhouse Firecracker Chicken	84
Margaritaville Jamaica Mistica Wings	86
Noodles and Company Spicy Asian Meatballs	88
McMenamins Cajun Tots	90
Panda Express Cream Cheese Wontons	91
Panera Bread Broccoli Cheese Soup	92
PF Chang's Bang Bang Shrimp	93
PF Chang's Chicken Lettuce Wraps	94

PF Chang's Hunan Dragon Wings	95
PF Chang's Spare Ribs	96
PF Chang's Spicy Green Beans	97
PF Chang's Crispy Green Beans	98
PF Chang's Dynamite Shrimp	99
Red Lobster Parrot Bay Coconut Shrimp	100
Red Lobster Bacon-Wrapped Stuffed Shrimp	102
Red Lobster Cheddar Bay Crab Bake	104
Red Lobster Seafood Stuffed Mushrooms	105
Red Robbin No-Fire Peppers	106
Ruth's Chris Barbecued Shrimp	108
Ruby Tuesday Thai Phoon Shrimp	110
Outback Steakhouse Alice Springs Quesadilla	112
Outback Steakhouse Blooming Onion	114
Outback Steakhouse Kookaburra Wings	116
Romano's Macaroni Grill Crispy Brussels Sprouts	118
Outback Steakhouse Gold Coast Coconut Shrimp	119
Olive Garden Buschetta	120
Olive Garden Stuffed Mushrooms	121
Olive Garden Toasted Ravioli	122
Olive Garden Mozzarella Fonduta	123
Sonic Extreme Tots	124
Simon Kitchen & Bar Wok-Charred Edamame	125
Taco Bell Mexican Pizza	126
Taco Bell Crunch Wrap Supreme	127
Texas Roadhouse Fried Pickles	128
Texas Roadhouse Rattlesnake Bites	130
TGI Friday's Potato Skins	131
TGI Friday's Pretzel Sticks and Beer Cheese Dip	132
TGI Friday's Crispy Green Bean Fries	134
TGI Fridays' BBQ Chicken Wings	136

Dips and Sauces

California Pizza Kitchen Tuscan Hummus

Prep Time: 30 minutes
Cooking Time: 30 minutes
Servings: 6

Ingredients

- 10 garlic cloves
- ½ cup tahini or sesame paste
- 2 cans great northern or cannellini beans, drained (15-ounce size)
- 1/8 teaspoon ground coriander
- 1 tablespoon plus ½ teaspoon soy sauce
- ¼ cup lemon juice, freshly squeezed
- 1 ½ teaspoon cumin
- ½ teaspoon cayenne pepper
- 2 tablespoons fresh Italian parsley, minced
- 1 ½ teaspoon salt
- ¼ cup cold water, if required

For California Pizza Kitchen Checca:
- 2 pounds Roma tomatoes, cut into ½" dice
- 1 tablespoon fresh basil, minced
- ½ cup extra-virgin olive oil
- 1 tablespoon garlic, minced
- 2 teaspoons salt

Directions

1. Process the garlic cloves in a food processor attached with a steel blade until minced finely, stopping & scrapping the sides of the work bowl occasionally, as required.
2. Add in the cannellini beans & pulse again until coarsely chopped. Then, with the machine still running on low speed, slowly pour the sesame paste through the feed tube & puree. Don't just turn off the motor; pour in the soy sauce, olive oil and lemon juice through the feed tube (stopping & scrapping down the sides, as required).
3. Stop; remove the lid & add cumin, cayenne, coriander and salt. Process again until blended thoroughly. Feel free to add ¼ to ½ cup of cold water to the mix and pulse, if the puree seems to be too thick for spreading or dipping. Transfer the puree to a large bowl & cover with a plastic wrap; let refrigerate until chill.
4. In the meantime; preheat your oven to 250 F in advance.
5. Place the pita breads in the preheated oven & heat for a couple of minutes, until thoroughly warmed.
6. Carefully remove the breads & cut into desired wedges. Place the chilled hummus in a serving bowl or plate & arrange the tomato Checca over the top. Garnish with the freshly chopped parsley & surround with the pita triangles. Serve immediately and enjoy.

For California Pizza Kitchen Checca
1. Toss the entire Checca ingredients together in a large-sized mixing bowl; continue to toss until thoroughly mixed. Using a plastic wrap; cover & refrigerate until ready to use.

Cheddar's Santa Fe Spinach Dip

Prep Time: 5 minutes
Cooking Time: 20 minutes
Servings: 6

Ingredients

- 2 packages chopped spinach, frozen (10 ounces each)
- 1 cup heavy whipping cream
- 2.4 ounces Monterey jack cheese; cut it into 3 equal 2" long blocks
- 1 package cream cheese (8 oz)
- 2.4 ounces pepper jack cheese; cut it into 3 equal 2" long blocks
- ½ cup Sour Cream
- 2.4 ounces White American Cheese; cut it into 3 equal 2" long blocks
- ½ to 1 teaspoon salsa seasoning
- 2 teaspoon Alfredo sauce
- 1 cup mozzarella cheese
- Pepper & salt to taste

Directions

1. Over low-heat in a large pan; heat the chopped spinach until all the moisture is cooked out, for a couple of minutes, stirring frequently.
2. In the meantime, over moderate heat in a large pot; add in the cream cheese & 1 cup of heavy whipping cream; cook until the cheese is completely melted; ensure that you don't really bring it to a boil. Feel free to decrease the heat, if it starts to boil.
3. Once done; work in batches and start adding the Pepper Jack, Monterey Jack & White American cheeses. Continue to stir the ingredients & don't let it come to a boil.
4. Lastly add in the Mozzarella cheese and continue to cook.
5. Add 2 teaspoons of the Alfredo sauce and then add in the cooked spinach.
6. Add ½ cup of the sour cream; continue to mix until combined well.
7. Add salsa seasoning, pepper & salt to taste; stir well
8. Serve immediately with some tortilla chips & enjoy!

Chevy's Mango Salsa

Prep Time: 20 minutes
Cooking Time: 2 minutes
Servings: 2 ⅓ cups

Ingredients

- 1 mango, peeled, seeded & diced (roughly 2 cups)
- 2 tablespoons red bell pepper, minced
- ¼ cup white onion, minced
- 1 teaspoon fresh cilantro, minced
- ½ teaspoon habanero pepper, finely minced
- 1 teaspoon lime juice, freshly squeezed
- 1/8 teaspoon salt

Directions

1. Combine the entire ingredients together in a medium-sized bowl; mix well until evenly combined. Using a plastic wrap; cover & let chill.
2. Serve chilled & enjoy

Carrabba's Bread Dipping Blend

Prep Time: 10 minutes
Cooking Time: 10 minutes
Servings: 8

Ingredients

- 1 tablespoon red pepper, crushed
- 1 ½ teaspoon garlic powder
- 1 tablespoon dried parsley
- ½ teaspoon dried rosemary
- 1 tablespoon dried basil
- 1 ½ teaspoon onion powder
- 1 tablespoon dried oregano
- 3 garlic cloves, fresh, crushed
- Extra virgin olive oil, as required
- 1 tablespoon freshly cracked black pepper
- 1 ½ teaspoon coarse sea salt

Directions

1. Combine black pepper together with the parsley, crushed red pepper, basil, oregano, onion powder, garlic powder, rosemary, crush garlic and sea salt; mix well.
2. Place the dry spice mixture in a large-sized shallow plate & drizzle with the extra virgin olive oil. Mix well & serve.

Chili's Salsa

Prep Time: 10 minutes
Cooking Time: 10 minutes
Servings: 12

Ingredients

- 1 can Tomatoes & Green Chilies, Diced (approximately 14.5 oz)
- ¼ teaspoon sugar
- 1 tablespoon canned jalapenos, diced
- ½ teaspoon cumin
- 1 teaspoon garlic, minced
- ¼ cup yellow onion, diced
- 1 can whole tomatoes plus juice (approximately 14.5 oz)
- 1 to 2 tablespoon fresh cilantro, chopped
- 1 tablespoon lime juice, freshly squeezed
- ½ teaspoon sea salt

Directions

1. Place onions and jalapenos in a food processor; pulse on high settings for a couple of seconds.
2. Add both cans of tomatoes together with lime juice, garlic, cumin, cilantro, sugar and salt to the food processor; process on high settings again until blended well (ensure that you don't puree it).
3. Using a plastic wrap; cover & let chill in a fridge or refrigerator for an hour before serving. Serve with your favorite tortilla chips and enjoy.

Cheesecake Factory Warm Crab & Artichoke Dip

Prep Time: 5 minutes
Cooking Time: 5 minutes
Servings: 2

Ingredients

For Crab Mix:
- 6 ounces artichoke hearts, drained & cut into ¾" pieces
- ¼ teaspoon Old Bay seasoning
- 1 slice of white bread, minced
- ¾ pounds crab meat (backfin or lump)
- 3 ounces cream cheese
- 1 cup heavy cream
- ¼ teaspoon ground black pepper
- 5 ounces sour cream
- ¼ teaspoon cayenne pepper
- 4 ounces mayonnaise
- ½ teaspoon kosher salt

For Bruschetta:
- 4 slices sourdough baguette, sliced ½" thick
- 2 teaspoons breadcrumbs, buttered & toasted
- 6 ounces Crab & Artichoke Mix
- 1 tablespoon olive oil
- ½ teaspoon parsley, chopped

Directions

For the Crab Mix:
1. Place the cream cheese and minced bread into a large-sized mixing bowl. Pour in the heavy cream & mix until evenly combined. Add the mayonnaise, cayenne pepper, sour cream, old bay seasoning, pepper and salt into the mixing bowl. Give them a good stir until combined evenly. Add in the crab meat, artichoke hearts and crab cake mix into the bowl. Gently "fold" into the other ingredients (ensure that you don't break up any large lump pieces of the crab)

For Bruschetta:
1. Evenly brush both sides of each bread slice with the olive oil. Place the bread onto a flat grill (over medium heat) & cook for a couple of minutes, until the slices turn lightly golden and have become crispy. Now, over moderate heat in a sauté pan; heat the crab & artichoke dip until it's warm throughout, stirring frequently to prevent burning.
2. Place the crab & artichoke dip into a small-sized serving bowl. Evenly sprinkle with the toasted buttered breadcrumbs. Slice each piece of grilled bread in half at a slight angle. Place the grilled bread slices and the bowl with crab dip onto a large-sized serving platter. Sprinkle freshly chopped parsley over the bread and crab dip. Serve and enjoy.

Joe's Crab Shack Blue Crab Dip

Prep Time: 5 minutes
Cooking Time: 25 minutes
Servings: 4

Ingredients

- 8 ounces softened cream cheese
- 2 teaspoons dry white wine
- 6 ounces lump crabmeat, drained
- 3 tablespoons evaporated milk or heavy whipping cream
- 2 teaspoons chicken soup base or shrimp soup base
- 3 tablespoons parmesan cheese, grated, divided
- 1 ½ tablespoons green or red bell peppers, diced
- 3 green onions, dark green ends & root ends trimmed, minced
- 2 teaspoons drained salsa or diced tomatoes
- ½ teaspoon Old Bay crab boil seasoning

Directions

1. Fold the entire ingredients (except 1 tablespoon Parmesan) together.
2. Evenly spread into an oven-proof baking dish and microwave for 4 minutes on half power.
3. Top with the Parmesan and transfer dish to the oven; broil for a couple of minutes, until the top turns out to be browned slightly.

Olive Garden Spinach-Artichoke Dip

Prep Time: 2 minutes
Cooking Time: 35 minutes
Servings: 10

Ingredients

- 1 can artichoke hearts, drained, coarsely chopped (14 ounce)
- ¼ cup mayonnaise
- 1 package light cream cheese (8 ounce); at room temperature
- ¼ cup parmesan cheese
- ½ cup chopped spinach, frozen
- ¼ cup Romano cheese
- 1 garlic clove, minced finely
- ¼ cup mozzarella cheese, grated
- ½ teaspoon dry basil or 1 tablespoon fresh
- ¼ teaspoon garlic salt
- Pepper & salt to taste

Directions

1. Combine cream cheese together with mayonnaise Romano cheese, Parmesan, basil, garlic & garlic salt; mix until combined well.
2. Add in the drained spinach and artichoke hearts; mix until well blended.
3. Spray a pie pan with Pam and then pour in the dip; top with the Mozzarella cheese.
4. Bake until the top is browned, for 25 minutes, at 350 F.
5. Serve with Italian or French toasted bread, thinly sliced.

Red Robin Campfire Sauce

Prep Time: 10 minutes
Cooking Time: 10 minutes
Servings: 6

Ingredients

- ½ cup mayo
- 1/8 teaspoon cayenne pepper
- ½ teaspoon paprika
- 1/8 teaspoon garlic powder
- ½ cup your favorite BBQ sauce

Directions

1. Whisk the entire ingredients together until completely smooth; serve immediately & enjoy.

Ruby Tuesday Queso Dip

Prep Time: 10 minutes
Cooking Time: 10 minutes
Servings: 6

Ingredients

- 1 box chopped spinach, frozen, thawed & squeeze out any excess water (approximately 10 oz)
- 1 jar of Taco Bell salsa & queso (approximately 14 oz)

Directions

1. Mix the entire ingredients together in a microwave-safe bowl. Heat in 1-minute intervals on high-power, stirring frequently. Continue to heat in the microwave until heated through. Serve with your favorite tortilla chips and enjoy.

Houston's Chicago Style Spinach Dip

Prep Time: 5 minutes
Cooking Time: 15 minutes
Servings: 10

Ingredients

- ⅓ cup sour cream
- 2 bags of fresh Spinach (1 pound each)
- ⅔ cup fresh parmesan cheese, grated
- 1 can Artichoke Hearts, coarsely diced
- 1/8 pound butter
- 2 tablespoons onions, minced
- ½ cup Monterrey Jack Cheese, grated
- 1 teaspoon fresh garlic, minced
- ½ teaspoon Tabasco sauce or to taste
- 1 pint heavy whipping cream
- ¼ cup flour
- 2 teaspoons lemon juice, freshly squeezed
- ½ teaspoon salt

Directions

1. Steam the spinach; strain & using a cheese cloth; squeeze the water out. Finely chop & set aside until ready to use.
2. Now, over moderate heat in a heavy saucepan; heat the butter until completely melted.
3. Add in the onions and garlic; sauté for 3 to 5 minutes.
4. Make a roux by adding the flour. Give everything a good stir & cook for a minute.
5. Slowly add in the heavy cream, stirring with a whisk to prevent lumping. The mixture would thicken at the boiling point.
6. When done, immediately add in the Tabasco, lemon juice, Parmesan cheese and salt.
7. Immediately remove the pan from heat & let stand at room temperature for 5 minutes and then stir in the sour cream.
8. Fold in the diced artichoke hearts, Jack cheese and dry & chopped spinach. Stir well until the cheese is completely melted.
9. Serve immediately and enjoy.

Margaritaville Crab, Shrimp and Mushroom Dip

Prep Time: 15 minutes
Cooking Time: 45 minutes
Servings: 8

Ingredients

For Bread:
- 2 loaves of Italian bread
- ½ teaspoon dried parsley flakes
- 1 stick of butter, melted (approximately ½ cup)
- ¼ teaspoon garlic powder

For Dip:
- 1 cup bay shrimp (smallest shrimp), cooked
- ¼ cup celery, minced
- 1 cup Monterey jack cheese, shredded
- ¼ cup onion, minced
- 1 teaspoon red pepper flakes, crushed
- 2 cups heavy cream
- 1 cup cheddar cheese, shredded
- 1 ½ cups white mushrooms, sliced
- 2 green onions, sliced
- 1 cup blue crab
- 2 tablespoons butter
- ¼ teaspoon salt

Directions

1. Over low heat in a large saucepan; heat 2 tablespoons of butter until completely melted and then add in the onions, celery & red pepper flakes. Let the ingredients to simmer slowly for 20 minutes, until the onions start to turn translucent & the celery softens, over low heat.
2. Add in the mushrooms, cream, shrimp, crab & salt to the hot pan. Increase the heat a bit and continue cooking until the liquid starts to bubble. Once done; decrease the heat & let the mixture to simmer until it decreases to approximately ½ of the volume & becomes thick. Keep an eye on the saucepan and ensure that the mixture doesn't bubble over. Meanwhile, crank the oven up to broil.
3. Now, cut the loaves into ½" thick slices. In a small-sized bowl; combine garlic powder together with dried parsley flakes and a stick of melted butter. Brush some of the garlic butter on each side of each slice of bread & toast under the hot broiler until the bread is toasted to a light brown, for a minute or two per side.
4. When the dip has thickened pour the mixture into an 8x8" casserole dish. Combine the shredded jack and cheddar cheese & sprinkle the cheese mixture on top of the dip. Broil until the cheese is completely melted, for 3 to 4 minutes. Sprinkle the sliced green onions on top & serve hot with the garlic toast on the side & some forks or spoons for spreading the dip onto the toast. Enjoy.

On the Border Guacamole Live

Prep Time: 30 minutes
Cooking Time: 10 minutes
Servings: 30

Ingredients

- 2 avocados, fresh
- 1 tablespoon fresh cilantro, chopped
- 2 tablespoon tomato, seeded & diced
- 1 tablespoon red onion, finely diced
- 1 ½ tablespoon Jalapenos, fresh, finely diced
- 1 Lime Wedge
- Salt to taste

Directions

1. Place the avocados in a large bowl & mash with a large fork until just chunky.
2. Squeeze the juice of lime into the avocado; mix well.
3. Add in the leftover ingredients & continue to mix until you get your desired consistency.

Olive Garden Hot Artichoke Spinach Dip

Prep Time: 30 minutes
Cooking Time: 30 minutes
Servings: 4

Ingredients

- ½ cup chopped spinach, frozen, thawed & well drained
- 1 package (8-ounce size) cream cheese, at room temperature
- ¼ cup each of Mozzarella cheese, Romano cheese & Parmesan cheese, shredded
- 1 garlic clove, minced finely
- ¼ cup mayonnaise
- 1 can artichoke hearts, drained & coarsely chopped (14 ounce)
- ½ teaspoon dried basil
- ¼ teaspoon garlic salt

Directions

1. Lightly grease a large-sized glass pie plate and preheat your oven to 350 F in advance.
2. Beat the cream cheese together with Romano cheese, Parmesan cheese, mayonnaise, basil, garlic & garlic salt in a large-sized mixing bowl; beat well.
3. Stir in the spinach and artichoke hearts until mixed well.
4. When ready, spoon the dip into the greased pie plate & evenly sprinkle the top with the Mozzarella cheese.
5. Place the dip in the oven and bake until the Mozzarella cheese is completely melted & turns lightly browned, for 25 minutes, at 350 F.
6. Remove the dip from oven & serve hot with some crackers or toasted bread slices for dipping.

Breads & Biscuits

Applebee's Pizza Sticks

Prep Time: 5 minutes
Cooking Time: 35 minutes
Servings: 3

Ingredients

- 1 loaf frozen bread dough; thaw & raised
- Melted Butter
- Pepperoni
- Italian Seasoning
- Garlic Powder
- Shredded Cheese
- Pizza Sauce

Directions

1. Spread the dough out into a jelly roll pan, well-greased & cut into desired sticks.
2. Brush the top with melted butter and then top with shredded cheese, pepperoni, garlic & Italian seasoning.
3. Bake until golden brown, for 25 to 30 minutes, at 350 F.
4. Cut the pizza sticks again, if required & serve with the pizza sauce.

Buca Di Beppo Garlic Bread

Prep Time: 5 minutes
Cooking Time: 20 minutes
Servings: 4

Ingredients

- 6 garlic cloves, thinly sliced or to taste
- 1 loaf of Italian bread; cut horizontally (fresh-baked)
- 2ounces garlic olive oil
- ¼ cup each of parmesan & mozzarella, freshly grated

Directions

1. Preheat your oven to 450 F in advance. Place the loaf halves on a cookie pan or sheet & generously brush the top of each half with garlic olive oil.
2. Evenly spread the sliced garlic over the loaf and then sprinkle with the parmesan cheese and mozzarella cheese; bake for 10 to 12 minutes, until turn lightly golden brown, at 450 F.
3. Remove & cut into 8 even-sized pieces. Once done; place the baked pieces of loaf in a basket lined with a napkin; serve & enjoy.

Little Caesar's Italian Bread Sticks

Prep Time: 15 minutes
Cooking Time: 30 minutes
Servings: 3

Ingredients

- 1 package instant yeast (2 ½ teaspoon)
- 3 tablespoon melted butter
- 22 ounces or 4 cups plus more bread flour
- 1 ½ teaspoons salt
- 3 tablespoon Parmesan cheese
- ½ cup warm water
- 2 tablespoon olive oil
- 1 ¼ cups water
- ½ teaspoon garlic salt

Directions

1. Whisk the yeast together with ½ cup of warm water in a medium-sized bowl. Give the yeast enough time to become active (bubble up). Once done; add oil and room temperature water to the yeast mixture; give everything a good stir until evenly combined. Pour flour & salt into the bowl of your food processor, pulse on high settings until combined well. Add olive oil, yeast & water through the tube & process until the dough is smooth & elastic. Place the dough into a bowl (coated lightly with the non-stick spray); cover the dough using a plastic wrap. Set aside for 2 hours & let rise until the dough has almost doubled in size.
2. Gently pat the dough out on a floured surface into a rectangular shape. Cut the dough into two equal portions down the middle and then make approximately 8 horizontal cuts across the dough. Coat a large-sized baking sheet with the non-stick spray and roll each portion of dough into a breadstick.
3. Bake until the breadsticks turn golden, for 16 to 18 minutes, at 375 F. Remove from the oven & set aside. Combine the melted butter with the garlic salt and brush the breadsticks with the garlic sauce. Sprinkle Parmesan cheese on top of the breadsticks.

Cheesecake Factory Sweet Corn Tamale Cakes

Prep Time: 1 hour & 15 minutes
Cooking Time: 20 minutes
Servings: 4

Ingredients

For Pico De Gallo:
- 1 Roma tomato, large, diced
- ½ teaspoon lime juice, freshly squeezed
- 1 tablespoon cilantro, fresh, minced
- Ground pepper & salt to taste
- 1 tablespoon red onion diced

For Salsa Verde:
- 2 tomatillos, chopped roughly
- 1 green onion, thinly sliced
- ¼ teaspoon ground cumin
- 1 can diced green chilies, drained (4-ounce)
- 2 tablespoons cilantro, fresh, chopped roughly
- 1/8 teaspoon ground black pepper
- 1 ½ teaspoons granulated sugar
- ¼ teaspoon salt

For Corn Cakes:
- 2 tablespoon all-purpose flour
- ½ cup softened butter, at room temperature
- 3 tablespoon sugar
- 1 ½ cups sweet corn, frozen
- ½ cup corn masa harina flour
- 1 ½ tablespoon olive oil
- 1/8 teaspoon salt

For Southwestern Sauce:
- ½ teaspoon granulated sugar
- 1 teaspoon white vinegar
- ½ teaspoon chili powder
- 1 teaspoon water
- ½ cup mayonnaise
- ¼ teaspoon paprika
- 1/8 teaspoon garlic powder

- ¼ teaspoon onion powder
- 1/8 teaspoon cayenne pepper

For Garnish:
- Avocado diced
- Fresh cilantro chopped
- Sour cream

Directions

For Pico De Gallo:
1. Place the entire ingredients together in a small bowl; toss until combined well. Cover & let chill for an hour.

For Salsa Verde:
1. Combine the entire ingredients together in a food processor. Pulse on high settings until combined well, but still a little chunky. Now, transfer the mixture to a small-sized bowl; cover & let chill for an hour.

For Southwestern Sauce:
1. Combine the entire ingredients together in a small-sized bowl until combined well. Cover & let chill for an hour.

For Corn Cakes:
1. Add a cup of frozen corn in a food processor and pulse until coarsely pureed. Add the pureed corn together with sugar, softened butter & salt in a medium-sized bowl. Mix until combined well.
2. Add in the masa & flour; mix until no flour streaks remain. Add in the leftover frozen corn kernels & mix until corn is distributed evenly.
3. Measure approximately ½ cup portions of the mixture out & make approximately 3" wide patties using your hands.
4. Now, over medium-low heat in a large skillet; heat the olive oil. Once hot; add the formed patties into the hot skillet & cook for 5 to 8 minutes, until turn golden brown. Carefully flip & cook the other side for 5 to 8 more minutes, until turns golden brown.

To Assemble:
1. Add & evenly spread the Salsa Verde to the platter. Heat the platter for a minute in the microwave. Place the corn cakes over the warmed Salsa Verde & distribute the Southwestern Sauce and Pico De Gallo evenly over the tops. Dollop with sour cream & garnish with avocado & cilantro. Serve immediately and enjoy.

Outback Steakhouse Honey Wheat Bushman

Prep Time: 15 minutes
Cooking Time: 1 hour & 30 minutes
Servings: 6 persons

Ingredients

- 2 cups bread flour
- 1 tablespoon granulated sugar
- 2 tablespoons softened butter
- ½ cup honey
- 1 teaspoon caramel coloring
- 2 cups wheat flour
- 1 tablespoon cocoa
- 2 ¼ teaspoon yeast
- 1 ½ teaspoon instant coffee granules
- 3 tablespoon cornmeal, for dusting
- 1 ½ cups warm water
- 1 teaspoon salt

Directions

1. Place the entire ingredients together in the bread machine & process on the dough setting. The dough will be a little sticky and wet on the side but add more of flour, if it appears to be too wet.
2. When done; set aside for an hour and let rise.
3. Remove from the pan; punch down & evenly divide into eight portions. Make approximately 2" wide & 6 to 8" long tubular shaped loaves from the portions.
4. Sprinkle the entire surface with cornmeal & place them on two cookie sheets.
5. Cover & let rise for an hour.
6. Bake for 20 to 25 minutes, at 350 F.
7. Serve warm with some whipped butter & enjoy.

Popeyes Buttermilk Biscuits

Prep Time: 30 minutes
Cooking Time: 30 minutes
Servings: 10 persons

Ingredients

- ¼ cup milk
- 2 cup unbleached all-purpose flour
- ½ teaspoon baking soda
- 1 tablespoon sugar
- ½ cup buttermilk
- 1 ½ teaspoon baking powder
- ½ cup unsalted butter, cold
- 1 ½ teaspoon salt
- Butter, to brush on top

Directions

1. Preheat your oven to 400 F in advance.
2. Mix the flour together with baking powder, baking soda, sugar & salt in a medium-sized bowl.
3. Slice the cold butter into cubes & cut the butter into dry mixture use a potato masher or pastry knife until no large chunks of the butter remain.
4. Add in the buttermilk & milk; give everything a good stir using a large wooden spoon until dough like consistency is achieved.
5. Roll out to ½" thick on a floured surface.
6. Cut the biscuits with a 3" biscuit cutter & arrange them on a baking sheet, lightly greased or lined with parchment paper.
7. Bake in the preheated oven until tops start to turn light brown, for 22 to 24 minutes.
8. Remove the biscuits from oven & let cool for a few minutes, then brush the top of each biscuit with the melted butter.

Pizza Hut Cheese Bread

Prep Time: 50 minutes
Cooking Time: 15 minutes
Servings: 20

Ingredients

For the Dough:
- 4 cups bread flour
- ¼ cup dry milk powder, non-fat
- 1⅓ cups warm water
- 2 ¼ teaspoon instant rapid-rise yeast
- 1 tablespoon granulated sugar
- 2 tablespoons olive oil
- ½ teaspoon salt

For the Dipping Sauce:
- ½ teaspoon garlic powder
- 1 can tomato sauce (5ounce)
- ½ teaspoon dried basil
- 1 teaspoon granulated sugar
- ½ teaspoon dried marjoram
- 1teaspoon dried oregano
- ¼ teaspoon salt

For Seasoning the Breadstick:
- 1 ¾ teaspoon garlic powder
- 1 tablespoon onion powder
- 12 tablespoon melted unsalted butter, divided
- 1 tablespoon dried oregano
- 2 tablespoons Parmesan cheese, grated
- 1 ½ teaspoon dried basil
- ½ teaspoon salt

Directions

For the Dough:
1. In the bowl of a stand mixer attached with the dough hook; place the sugar together with dry milk powder, yeast & salt. Add in the water; give everything a good stir until evenly mixed. Let sit for 2 to 5 minutes, until the mixture begins to bubble. Add in the olive oil & stir again.
2. Slowly add in the flour and process on low speed until dough starts forming. Increase the speed to medium-low & continue kneading for 5 more minutes, until soft and slightly tacky dough forms. Turn the dough out onto a lightly floured surface & divide into two portions.
3. Coat the bottoms of 2 pans, 9x13" with 4 tablespoons of melted butter. Roll each piece of dough into a 9x13" rectangle & fit in the bottom of each pan; brushing the tops with 1 tablespoon of the melted butter. Tightly wrap in the plastic wrap & place in a warm, dust-free area for 1 ½ hours, until puffed & nearly doubled in size.

For the Dipping Sauce:
1. Stir the tomato sauce together with marjoram, sugar, basil, oregano, garlic powder & salt in a small saucepan.
2. Place it over medium heat and cook for 30 minutes (the moment the sauce starts boiling, immediately decrease the heat to low & let simmer for the remaining time), stirring every now and then. Remove the pan from heat.
3. Preheat your oven to 475 F in advance.
4. Once the dough has risen, immediately get rid of the plastic wrap & using a pizza cutter; score each pan of the dough into 10 equal breadsticks.
5. Bake in the preheated oven for 10 to 15 minutes, until the edges start appearing crisp and turn golden brown.
6. In the meantime, prepare the breadstick seasoning. Stir the Parmesan cheese together with garlic powder, oregano, onion powder, basil & salt in a small bowl; stir well until evenly mixed.
7. As soon as you remove breadsticks from the oven, immediately brush them with the leftover melted butter and then sprinkle with the breadstick seasoning. Let cool for 5 to 10 minutes in the pan and then slide the breadsticks out onto a cutting board using a spatula.
8. Using a pizza cutter or knife; slice the breadsticks into desired shapes. Serve warm with the dipping sauce and enjoy.

Red Lobster Cheddar Bay Biscuits

Prep Time: 15 minutes
Cooking Time: 20 minutes
Servings: 16 persons

Ingredients

- 3 cup all-purpose flour
- 2 teaspoon garlic powder
- 1 ¾ cup whole milk
- 2 tablespoon baking powder
- 1 ½ cup sharp cheddar, shredded
- ½ cup butter
- 1 tablespoon parsley, freshly chopped
- 1 ½ sticks cold butter, chopped
- 1 teaspoon garlic powder
- ¼ teaspoon kosher salt

Directions

1. Preheat your oven to 400 F in advance.
2. In a large-sized mixing bowl; combine flour together with baking powder, butter and salt using an electric mixer (starting from slow & then increase the speed to medium) until dough forms with pea-sized lumps. With the motor still running on low-speed, slowly add in the milk.
3. Fold in the cheese and garlic powder. Place 2" blobs of dough onto a baking sheet lined with parchment using a spoon. Bake in the preheated oven for 18 to 20 more minutes, until lightly golden.
4. Melt the butter in the microwave, in 20-second intervals, stirring frequently, until melted completely. Stir in the garlic powder and parsley. As soon as the biscuit are out from the oven; immediately brush the mixture on top of each biscuit. Serve immediately & enjoy.

More Appetizers

Abuelo Jalapeno Poppers

Prep Time: 10 minutes
Cooking Time: 1 hour & 10 minutes
Servings: 8 persons

Ingredients

- 30 jalapeno peppers; sliced into half lengthwise
- 1 cup milk
- 2 packages soften cream cheese, at room temperature (8-ounces each)
- 1/8 teaspoon paprika
- 12 ounces Cheddar cheese, shredded
- 1/8 teaspoon chili powder
- 1 cup flour
- 1/8 teaspoon garlic powder
- 1 cup seasoned bread crumbs
- ¼ teaspoon ground black pepper
- 1 quart of oil for frying
- ¼ teaspoon salt

Directions

1. Scrape out seeds and the pith inside of the jalapeno peppers using a spoon. Combine cheddar cheese together with cream cheese in a medium-sized bowl; give them a good stir until blended well. Fill each pepper half with the prepared cream cheese blend using a spoon.
2. Add flour into a small-sized shallow bowl. Add paprika, pepper, garlic powder, chili powder and salt. Blend into the flour until it is mixed. Pour milk into a separate medium-sized shallow bowl. Dip stuffed jalapeno into flour.. Place the floured pepper on a large-sized baking sheet with a rack. Let dry for 10 minutes.
3. Pour the dried bread crumbs into a separate bowl. Dip the floured jalapeno pepper into the milk & then into the bowl with the bread crumbs. Place the pepper on the rack again. Preheat the oil to 350 F in advance. Dip pepper into the milk & then into the bread crumbs. Repeat these steps until you have utilized the entire dipping peppers.
4. Work in batches and fry peppers for a minute or two, until turn golden brown. Remove from oil & place them on a baking rack to drain.

Applebee's Chicken Wings

Prep Time: 15 minutes
Cooking Time: 35 minutes
Servings: 6

Ingredients

- 35 chicken wings
- 1 ½ tablespoon flour
- 3 tablespoons vinegar
- 1 ¼ teaspoon cayenne pepper
- 1 tablespoon Worcestershire sauce
- 12 ounces Louisiana hot sauce
- ¼ teaspoon garlic powder

Directions

1. Cook the chicken wings either by deep-frying or baking.
2. Mix the entire sauce ingredients (except the flour) together over low-medium heat in a large saucepan. Cook until warm and then add in the flour; stir well until you get your desired level of thickness.
3. When thick; cover the bottom of 9x13" baking dish with the sauce. Combine the leftover sauce with the cooked wings & place them in the baking dish. Bake until warm, for 15 to 20 minutes, at 300 F.
4. Serve with blue-cheese dressing and celery sticks. Enjoy.

Applebee's Baja Potato Boats

Prep Time: 10 minutes
Cooking Time: 30 minutes
Servings: 4

Ingredients

For Pico de Gallo:
- 1 ½ teaspoon fresh cilantro, minced
- 1 tablespoon canned jalapeño slices (nacho slices), diced
- 3 tablespoons Spanish onion, chopped
- 1 chopped tomato (approximately ½ cup)
- A dash each of freshly-ground black pepper & salt

For the Potato Boats:
- 2 slices Canadian bacon diced (roughly 2 tablespoons)
- Canola oil nonstick cooking spray, as required
- ⅓ cup Cheddar cheese, shredded
- 3 russet potatoes, medium
- ⅓ cup Mozzarella cheese
- salt as needed

On the Side:
- Salsa & sour cream

Directions

1. Combine the entire Pico De Gallo ingredients together in a large bowl; mix well. When done, place in a refrigerator until ready to use.
2. Preheat your oven to 400 F in advance. Place potatoes in oven & bake until tender, for an hour. Set aside at room temperature until easy to handle. When done, cut them lengthwise 2 times. This should make 3 ½ to ¾" slices; throwing the middle slices away.
3. Increase your oven's temperature to 450 F. Take a spoon & scoop out the inside of the potato skins. Ensure that you must leave at least ¼ of an inch of the potato inside each skin. Spray the potato skin completely on all sides with the spray of nonstick canola oil. Put the skins, cut-side facing up on a large-sized cookie sheet. Sprinkle them with salt & bake in the preheated oven until the edges start to turn brown, for 12 to 15 minutes.
4. Combine both the cheeses together in a large bowl. Sprinkle approximately 1 ½ tablespoons of the mixture on each potato skin. Then sprinkle a teaspoon of the Canadian bacon over the cheese. Top this with a large tablespoon of the pico de gallo and then sprinkle each skin with some more of cheese.
5. Place the skins into the oven again & bake until the cheese melts, for 2 to 4 more minutes. Remove & let them sit for a minute. Slice each one lengthwise using a sharp knife. Serve hot with some salsa and sour cream on the side.

Applebee's Onion Peels with Dipping Sauce

Prep Time: 35 minutes
Cooking Time: 45 minutes
Servings: 4 persons

Ingredients

For Onion Peels:
- 1 cup all-purpose flour
- 2 Vidalia onions, large
- 1 cup bread crumbs
- 2 to 2 ½ cups milk
- 1 teaspoon fresh ground black pepper
- Oil for frying
- 1 teaspoon salt or to taste

For Creamy Horseradish Dipping Sauce:
- ½ cup mayonnaise
- 2 teaspoons white distilled vinegar
- 1/8 teaspoon cayenne
- 1 teaspoon ketchup
- 1/8 teaspoon dried oregano
- 1 tablespoon prepared horseradish
- ¼ to ½ teaspoon medium grind black pepper
- 1 teaspoon paprika
- 1/8 teaspoon garlic powder
- 1 teaspoon water
- 1/8 teaspoon onion powder

Directions

For the Onion Peels:
1. Over moderate heat in a deep fryer or deep sauce pan; heat the oil until hot.
2. Slice and remove both ends from the onion.
3. Place the onion, flat side down on your cutting board & cut in ½ down the middle. Cut each ½ into 4 to 5 wedges more.
4. For onion petals; separate the onion pieces & layers.
5. Combine the entire dry ingredients together in a medium-sized bowl.
6. Whisk in 2 cups milk & blend until you get smooth batter like consistency. If required, feel free to add more of milk. Let sit until thickens slightly, for 5 more minutes and then whisk again.
7. Dip each individual onion petal in the prepared batter. Gently shaking to get rid of the excess batter & then carefully drop into the hot oil. Cook approximately 8 to 12 of the petals at one time.
8. Fry until turn light brown, for a minute or two, stirring gently.
9. Remove & place them on a plate covered with a paper towel to drain.
10. Repeat these steps until you have utilized the petals completely.
11. Serve with some Creamy Horseradish Dipping Sauce on side and enjoy.

For Creamy Horseradish Dipping Sauce
1. Whisk the entire dipping sauce ingredients together in a medium-sized bowl; whisk well until creamy. Cover & let chill in a refrigerator until ready to use.

Bahama Breeze West Indies Patties

Prep Time: 10 minutes
Cooking Time: 1 hour & 5 minutes
Servings: 6 persons

Ingredients

For Dough:
- 2 cups all-purpose flour
- ¼ cup whole milk
- 1 beaten egg, large
- ¼ cup cold salted butter
- 1 beaten egg, large
- ¼ cup vegetable shortening
- 6 to 10 cups vegetable oil
- ¾ teaspoon salt

For Filling:
- ½ pound ground beef, not lean
- 2 tablespoons chopped yellow onion
- ¼ cup russet potato, diced
- 1/8 teaspoon ground cayenne pepper
- 1 teaspoon minced parsley
- ¼ cup carrot, julienned
- ½ teaspoon lime juice, freshly squeezed
- 1 teaspoon curry powder
- ½ teaspoon paprika
- 2 tablespoons chicken broth
- ¼ teaspoon salt

For Apple-Mango Salsa:
- 1 tablespoon red bell pepper, minced
- 1 tablespoon lime juice, freshly squeezed
- 1 cup Granny Smith apple, finely diced
- 1 tablespoon jalapeno, minced
- 1 cup mango, finely diced
- 1 tablespoon fresh cilantro, minced
- A pinch of salt

For Seasoned Sour Cream:
- 1 cup sour cream
- ¼ cup tomato, diced
- 1 tablespoon red bell pepper, minced
- ¼ teaspoon ground cayenne pepper
- 1 tablespoon fresh cilantro, chopped
- A pinch of ground cumin
- 1 tablespoon red onion, chopped
- ¼ teaspoon salt

Directions

For Dough:
1. Combine the flour with salt in a large-sized mixing bowl. Add in the cold butter and shortening; cut them into the flour use a pastry knife.
2. Add in the milk and beaten egg; give everything a good stir until evenly combined. Form the dough into a ball using your hands. Wrap in a plastic wrap & let refrigerate until you prepare the filling.

For Filling:
1. Over medium heat in a large skillet; brown the ground beef. As it cooks; don't forget to break it into small pieces. Once done; using a large-sized slotted spoon; immediately remove the ground beef from skillet & set aside; leaving the fat in the skillet.
2. Place & potatoes in a small-sized saucepan and fill the pan with water (enough to cover). Bring it to a boil over moderate heat. Once done, drain the potato & place them in the skillet along with onion and carrot. Sauté over medium heat for 3 to 4 minutes.
3. Add ground beef to the skillet again along with paprika, curry powder, parsley, cayenne pepper and salt. Stir in the lime juice & chicken broth; let simmer for 3 to 4 more minutes. Turn off the heat & set aside.

For Apple-Mango Salsa:
1. Combine the entire salsa ingredients together in a medium-sized bowl & refrigerate until ready to use.

For Seasoned Sour Cream:

1. Combine the entire ingredients together in a small-sized bowl & refrigerate until ready to use.
2. Roll the dough out on a lightly floured surface until very flat. Cut circles out of the dough using an upside-down cup or glass with a diameter of approximately 4 ½".
3. Paint the egg around the edges of dough using a pastry brush. Place a heaping tablespoon of the filling in middle & fold dough over; pressing the edges to seal. Ensure that you press out any air as well. Press along the edges using a fork.
4. Place the patties in a large zip-top bag & place in the freezer for a couple of hours.
5. Heat the oil in a Dutch oven to 375 F. Work in batches & fry the patties (4 at a time) until turn golden brown, for 5 to 6 minutes. Flip halfway through the cooking time.
6. Serve with sour cream and salsa.

Applebee's Chicken Quesadilla

Prep Time: 15 minutes
Cooking Time: 35 minutes
Servings: 6 persons

Ingredients

- ½ teaspoon dried oregano
- 2 ½ cups cooked chicken, shredded
- ¾ to 1 teaspoon ground cumin
- 6 flour tortillas (8" each)
- ¼ cup melted butter
- 2 cups Monterey Jack cheese, shredded
- ⅔ cup salsa
- Guacamole & sour cream
- ⅓ cup green onions, sliced
- ½ teaspoon salt

Directions

1. Combine the cooked chicken together with sliced green onions, salsa, dried oregano, ground cumin & salt in a large skillet. Cook over medium heat until heated through, for 8 to 10 minutes, uncovered, stirring occasionally.
2. Brush one side of the tortillas with melted butter; place the buttered side down on a baking sheet, lightly greased. Spoon approximately ⅓ cup of the chicken mixture over half of each tortilla and then sprinkle with approximately ⅓ cup of the cheese.
3. Fold the plain side of tortilla over the cheese & bake until golden brown and turn crisp, for 10 to 12 minutes, at 375 F. Cut into wedges; serve with guacamole and sour cream. Enjoy.

Bar Louie Loaded Tots

Prep Time: 15 minutes
Cooking Time: 50 minutes
Servings: 12 servings

Ingredients

- 7 ounces fresh bulk spicy pork sausage or chorizo
- 1 package frozen Tater Tots (approximately 32 ounces)
- 12 ounces process cheese (Velveeta), cubed
- 1 can diced tomatoes with mild green chilies, un-drained (14 ½ ounces)
- ½ cup jalapeno slices, pickled
- 1 can black beans, rinsed & drained (15 ounces)
- ¼ cup fresh cilantro, minced
- 1 ripe avocado, medium, cubed
- ⅓ cup green onions, thinly sliced
- 1 tomato, medium, chopped
- ½ cup sour cream

Directions

1. Preheat your oven to 425 F in advance. Place the Tater Tots in an ungreased 13x9" baking dish. Bake in the preheated oven for 35 to 40 minutes, uncovered.
2. In the meantime, over medium heat in a large skillet; cook the chorizo for a couple of minutes, until no longer pink from inside; breaking up into crumbles; drain. Remove from the pan & set aside. Add diced tomatoes & cheese in the same skillet. Cook over medium heat until the cheese is completely melted and well blended, uncovered, stirring occasionally. Pour the mixture on top of the Tater Tots. Sprinkle with the black beans and chorizo.
3. Bake for 10 more minutes, uncovered. Sprinkle with jalapenos, green onions and cilantro. Top with tomato and avocado. Serve with some sour cream on side and enjoy.

Benigan's Chicken Quesadillas

Prep Time: 10 minutes
Cooking Time: 30 minutes
Servings: 4

Ingredients

- 2-3 boneless skinless chicken breasts, diced
- 1 ripe tomato, large
- ½ onion
- 8 flour tortillas
- Spreadable butter
- ½ package old el paso fajita seasoning mix
- 1 pound mozzarella cheddar blend cheese, shredded
- ¼ cup water
- Pace cilantro salsa, to taste

Directions

1. Generously coat a pan with the olive oil or cooking spray and heat it over moderate heat. Once hot; add in the chicken pieces & fry.
2. Once chicken is fried, add water & seasoning to the hot pan.
3. Continue cooking for a couple of more minutes, until the sauce thickens slightly.
4. Set chicken & sauce aside and preparing the remaining ingredients.
5. Butter one side of the entire tortillas & set aside.
6. Dice the onion and the tomato, mix well & set aside.
7. Place a tortilla on a hot griddle or pan, buttered side down.
8. Layer the ingredients on the tortilla in the following order: cheese followed by the chicken & sauce then the onion-tomato mixture, cheese and lastly the salsa.
9. Top with one more tortilla, buttered side up.
10. Once the cheese begins to bubble from the sides of the quesadilla; carefully flip it using a spatula underneath (in one hand) and some tongs to hold the quesadilla together (in the other hand).
11. Continue to cook until the shell turns a bit crunchy & golden in color.
12. Let stand for a couple of minutes and then cut into quarters. Serve immediately with your favorite guacamole, sour cream or salsa for dipping. Enjoy.

Benihana Spicy Edamame

Prep Time: 5 minutes
Cooking Time: 20 minutes
Servings: 6

Ingredients

- ½ teaspoon garlic powder
- 1 package edamame pods, frozen (16 ounces)
- ¼ teaspoon red pepper flakes, crushed
- 2 teaspoon kosher salt
- ¾ teaspoon ground ginger

Directions

1. Place the edamame pods in a large saucepan & fill it with water (enough to cover). Bring everything together to a boil over moderate heat. Cover & cook for 4 to 5 minutes, until tender; drain. Transfer the cooked edamame pods to a large-sized serving bowl. Sprinkle with the seasonings; toss several times until evenly coated. Serve and enjoy.

BJ's Restaurant Avocado Wraps

Prep Time: 15 minutes
Cooking Time: 20 minutes
Servings: 9 persons

Ingredients

- 2 tablespoon sun-dried tomatoes in oil, drained & roughly chopped
- Juice of one lime, freshly squeezed
- 4 ounces cream cheese, fat-free, softened (½ package)
- ¼ cup red onion, minced
- 2 large, ripe avocados, diced
- A pinch of red pepper flakes
- 2 tablespoon fresh cilantro, chopped
- 1 garlic clove, minced
- 9 egg roll wrappers
- Cooking spray
- 1 tablespoon pine nuts, chopped
- Pepper & salt to taste

Directions

1. Line a large-sized baking sheet with the parchment paper; set aside & preheat your oven to 400 F in advance.
2. Place the diced avocados in a medium-sized bowl and then gently stir in the freshly squeezed lime juice.
3. Stir in the sun-dried tomatoes, cream cheese, onion, pine nuts, garlic, red pepper, cilantro, pepper and salt until combined thoroughly.
4. Lay an egg roll wrapper on a clean work surface. Place a few tablespoons of the avocado mixture down the middle of the wrapper. Fold one point of the wrapper over the mixture & roll once. Fold in the two sides & roll the egg roll shut. Fold in & seal the leftover tip using a bit of water. Place them on the prepared baking sheet & repeat with the leftover wrappers & filling ingredients.
5. Lightly coat the tops of your egg rolls with cooking spray & bake in the preheated oven for 8 to 10 minutes. Turn each egg roll & lightly coat the other side with the cooking spray as well. Place it to the oven & bake until browned & hot, for 10 more minutes.
6. Serve with your favorite dipping sauce & enjoy.

BJ's Restaurant Sriracha Brussels Sprouts

Prep Time: 5 minutes
Cooking Time: 35 minutes
Servings: 4 persons

Ingredients

- 1 ½ pounds Brussels sprouts; remove the stem ends & pulling any yellow outer leaves off and then cut large sprouts into half
- 3 tablespoons honey
- 1 tablespoon sriracha
- Juice of 1 lime, freshly squeezed
- 2 tablespoons olive oil
- Kosher salt to taste

Directions

1. Preheat your oven to 400 F in advance.
2. Place the sprouts in a large-sized bowl and then drizzle with the olive oil; generously season with the kosher salt to taste; toss several times until evenly coated. Place them on the baking sheet lined with an aluminum foil in a single layer. Roast in the preheated oven for 35 to 40 minutes, until tender on the inside and crisp & golden brown on the outside; during the cooking process, don't forget to shake the pan a couple of times.
3. In the meantime, combine honey together with sriracha & lime in a small-sized bowl. Season with the kosher salt.
4. Remove the sprouts from oven and transfer them to a large bowl; drizzle with the sauce. Lightly toss to coat & serve immediately. Enjoy.

BJ's Restaurant Root Beer Glazed Ribs

Prep Time: 10 minutes
Cooking Time: 8 hours & 25 minutes
Servings: 5 persons

Ingredients

- 4 ½ pounds pork baby back ribs; cut into 5 serving-sized pieces
- 1 cup root beer
- ¼ cup orange juice
- 1 cup ketchup
- ½ teaspoon ground ginger
- 3 tablespoons Worcestershire sauce
- 1 teaspoon onion powder
- ½ teaspoon paprika
- 2 tablespoons molasses
- ¼ teaspoon red pepper flakes, crushed
- 1 teaspoon garlic powder
- ½ teaspoon pepper
- 1 teaspoon salt

Directions

1. Over moderate heat in a small saucepan; combine the entire ingredients (except the meat, pepper & salt); mix well. Bring everything together to a boil. Once done; immediately decrease the heat & let simmer until the sauce is reduced to approximately 2 cups, for 8 to 10 minutes, uncovered; set aside.
2. Sprinkle the ribs pieces with pepper and salt. Place in a slow cooker, 5 or 6 quarts. Pour the prepared sauce on top of the ribs. Cover & cook until meat is tender, for 6 to 8 hours on low-heat. Serve with the sauce and enjoy.

Bonefish Grill Bang Bang Shrimp

Prep Time: 10 minutes
Cooking Time: 25 minutes
Servings: 4 persons

Ingredients

- 1 pound shrimp, shelled & deveined
- ¼ cup Thai sweet chili sauce
- ½ cup mayonnaise
- ¼ teaspoon Sriracha
- ¾ cup cornstarch
- ½ cup buttermilk
- Canola oil for frying

Directions

1. Add mayonnaise together with Sriracha and Thai sweet chili sauce in a small-sized bowl; give them a good stir until evenly mixed.
2. Add shrimp & buttermilk in a separate bowl; stir well until the shrimp is evenly coated.
3. Remove from the buttermilk & let any excess liquid to drain away.
4. Now, coat the shrimp in the cornstarch.
5. Hot a few inches of the canola oil over moderate heat in a heavy bottomed pan.
6. Fry the shrimp for 1 to 2 minutes per side, until brown lightly.
7. Once fried coat with the sauce & serve immediately.

Buca di Beppo World Famous Meatball

Prep Time: 10 minutes
Cooking Time: 55 minutes
Servings: 6 persons

Ingredients

- 1 ½ pounds ground chuck
- 2 eggs, large
- ¼ cup shredded parmesan cheese
- 6 garlic cloves
- ½ cup Italian bread crumbs
- 32 ounces authentic marinara sauce
- 1 teaspoon each of pepper and salt
- 8 ounces water

Directions

1. Preheat your oven to 350 F in advance. Combine the entire ingredients (except the Marinara Sauce) in a large-sized mixing bowl & thoroughly mix; ensure that you don't over mix the ingredients. Evenly divide the mixture into portions & make roughly 6 meatballs. Place the meatballs on a large-sized baking sheet sprayed with the cooking spray. Bake in the preheated oven for 12 to 15 minutes, until a dark brown crust forms.
2. Transfer the meatballs to a Dutch oven. Combine marinara sauce with water & pour on top of the meatballs. Cover the dish with an aluminum foil & bake for 35 to 45 more minutes, until meatballs are cooked through. Place the meatballs on a large platter. Skim the oil from the top of the marinara & ladle it on top of the meatballs.

Buffalo Wild Wings Ultimate Nachos

Prep Time: 25 minutes
Cooking Time: 15 minutes
Servings: 12

Ingredients

- 1 pound ground beef
- 2 plum tomatoes, chopped
- 1 jar salsa con queso dip (15 ½ ounces)
- ¾ cup water
- 1 cup refried beans
- ¼ cup fresh chives, minced
- 1 package tortilla chips (13 ounces)
- An envelope of taco seasoning
- ½ cup sour cream

Directions

1. Preheat your oven to 350 F in advance. Over moderate heat in a large skillet; cook & crumble the beef for 5 to 7 minutes, until no longer pink; drain. Stir in the taco seasoning & water; bring everything together to a boil. Once done; decrease the heat & let simmer for 5 minutes, until thickened, uncovered, stirring occasionally.
2. Layer a third of each of chips, beans, beef mixture & queso dip in an ungreased 13x9" baking pan. Repeat the layers two more times.
3. Bake in the preheated oven for 12 to 15 minutes, until heated through, uncovered. Top with tomatoes & chives; serve immediately with some sour cream on the side and enjoy.

Carraba's Italian Grill Zucchini Frittes

Prep Time: 25 minutes
Cooking Time: 25 minutes
Servings: 4 persons

Ingredients

- ¼ teaspoon ground chipotle pepper
- 2 zucchini, medium-sized; Cut each in half lengthwise & then in half crosswise. Cutting each piece lengthwise into ¼" slices
- ½ teaspoon garlic powder
- 1 cup Japanese panko bread crumbs
- ⅓ cup all-purpose flour
- 2 teaspoons smoked paprika
- ¾ cup Parmesan cheese, grated
- 2 large eggs, beaten
- ¼ teaspoon pepper
- 3 tablespoons olive oil
- ¼ teaspoon salt

Directions

1. Preheat your oven to 425 F in advance.
2. Combine bread crumbs together with cheese & seasonings in a shallow bowl. Place eggs and flour in separate shallow bowls.
3. Dip the zucchini slices first into the flour and then into the egg & then into the crumb mixture; patting to help coating adhere.
4. Arrange them on a greased rack in a rimmed baking pan lined with an aluminum foil. Drizzle with the oil & bake in the preheated oven for 20 to 25 minutes, until golden brown.

Cheddars Scratch Kitchen Texas Cheese Fries

Prep Time: 25 minutes
Cooking Time: 35 minutes
Servings: 4

Ingredients

- 6-8 slices of bacon; enough to make approximately ½ cup once cooked
- 4 cups steak fries, frozen
- ¼ teaspoon onion powder
- 2 cups sharp cheddar cheese, grated
- ¼ teaspoon seasoned salt
- Oil for frying, as required
- ¼ teaspoon garlic salt

Directions

1. Preheat your oven to 450 F in advance. Over medium-high heat in a medium-sized frying pan; cook the bacon until crisp.
2. Remove & place dry it on a paper towel. Pour the bacon grease into a bowl & let slightly cool. Add in the onion powder, seasoned salt & garlic salt to the grease; give everything a good stir until evenly mixed; set aside.
3. Arrange the fries on a lightly greased baking sheet & bake in the preheated oven until slightly golden, for 10 to 15 minutes.
4. Set the oven to broil settings. Brush the bacon with oil & seasoning mix onto each fry. Place the fries in an oven-safe bowl.
5. Spread the cheddar cheese on top of the fries. Crumble the bacon slices and then sprinkle on top of the cheese. Place the dish inside the oven and cook until the cheese is bubbly, for 5 more minutes. Remove & let sit for a couple of minutes. Serve immediately and enjoy.

Cheesecake Factory Tamale Cakes

Prep Time: 5 minutes
Cooking Time: 15 minutes
Servings: 4

Ingredients

- 2 cans cream style corn
- ¼ cup sugar
- 2 large eggs
- ½ cup milk
- 1 small package Jiffy Corn mix
- Coconut oil for frying
- ½ cup oil

Directions

1. Mix the entire ingredients together in a large bowl until you get dough like consistency.
2. Now, over medium-low heat in a large skillet; heat 1 tablespoon of the coconut oil.
3. Pour approximately ⅓ cup of the prepared batter into the hot skillet & cook until the cake starts to turn brown & cooked throughout, for approximately 2 minutes per side.
4. Continue this step until you have utilized the batter completely.

Cheesecake Factory Mini Crab Cakes

Prep Time: 15 minutes
Cooking Time: 55 minutes
Servings: 6 persons

Ingredients

- ½ pound lump crab meat
- 3 tablespoons plain bread crumbs
- ½ beaten egg
- 2 tablespoons green onion, minced (only green part)
- 1 teaspoon fresh parsley, minced
- 2 tablespoons mayonnaise
- ¼ cup Japanese panko breadcrumbs
- 2 tablespoons red bell pepper, minced
- 1 teaspoon Old Bay seasoning
- Vegetable oil, as required
- ½ teaspoon yellow prepared mustard

For Remoulade Sauce:
- 2 teaspoons capers
- ¼ teaspoon cayenne pepper
- ½ teaspoon fresh parsley, minced
- 2 teaspoons dill pickle slices, chopped
- ½ teaspoon paprika
- 1 teaspoon lemon juice
- ½ cup mayonnaise
- ¼ teaspoon ground cumin
- ½ teaspoon chili powder
- 1/8 teaspoon salt

Directions

1. Measure the entire ingredients for the crab cakes (except the vegetable oil and panko) into a large-sized bowl. Carefully fold the ingredients together using a large spatula. Ensure that you don't over stir the ingredients.
2. Fill six cups of a clean muffin tin with evenly with the crab mixture using a spoon or your hands. Press a bit on each crab cake down until the top is flat; make sure that you don't press them too hard. Cover the muffin tin with a plastic wrap & pop it inside the fridge for a few hours.
3. In the meantime; prepare the remoulade sauce by mixing the entire ingredients in a small-sized bowl. Cover & let the sauce to chill until ready to serve.
4. After a few hours; heat up approximately ¼" of the vegetable oil over medium to low heat in large skillet. Fill a shallow bowl with the panko breadcrumbs.
5. Carefully turn the crab cakes out onto a clean plate. Gently roll each crab cake around in the panko breadcrumbs.
6. Sauté the crab cakes in the hot oil until the cakes turn golden brown, for 1 ½ to 3 minutes per side.
7. Place the crab cakes on paper towels to drain and serve hot with the remoulade sauce alongside in a little dish.

Cheesecake Factory Avocado Eggrolls

Prep Time: 15 minutes
Cooking Time: 15 minutes
Servings: 12

Ingredients

For Dipping Sauce:
- 4 teaspoons white vinegar
- 1 cup cilantro, fresh
- ½ cup honey
- 1 teaspoon balsamic vinegar
- 2-5 garlic cloves
- 1 tablespoon white granulated sugar
- ½ cup cashews, chopped
- 1 teaspoon ground black pepper
- 2 green onions chopped
- ¼ teaspoon saffron, powdered
- 1 teaspoon ground cumin
- ½ cup olive oil or as required

For Egg Rolls:
- 8 tablespoons sun-dried tomatoes packed in oil, chopped
- 2 tablespoons chopped cilantro, fresh
- 3 avocados large, peeled, pitted & diced
- Egg roll wraps
- 3 tablespoons red onion, minced
- 1 beaten egg, large
- ¼ teaspoon salt

Directions

For the Avocado Rolls:
1. Gently stir the diced avocados together with onion, chopped sun-dried tomatoes, cilantro & salt in a large bowl.
2. Place one egg roll on a clean, large cutting board (ensure that the corner is pointing toward you). Brush the edges of the wrapper with the egg mixture.
3. Evenly distribute the prepared avocado filling onto the middle.
4. Fold the bottom corner up, ¼ of the way over the filling. Rolling up from side to side and then fold the top corner over all; pressing to seal.
5. Repeat with the leftover egg roll wrappers.
6. Now, over medium-high heat in a deep pan; heat the oil (enough to submerge a batch of avocado egg rolls).
7. Work in batches & deep fry the egg rolls until golden brown, for 3 to 4 minutes.
8. Remove the rolls from oil & place them on paper towels to drain.
9. Serve with some dipping sauce on side and enjoy.

For the Dipping Sauce:
1. Stir vinegars together with honey and saffron powder in a small, microwave safe bowl; microwave for a minute. Give everything a good stir & set the mixture aside.
2. Add to a blender along with the honey mixture and the remaining sauce ingredients. Puree on high settings until fully blended & combined well.
3. Pour the mixture into a bowl & stir in more of olive oil to thin it out, if required. Refrigerate until ready to use.

Chili's Southwest Egg Rolls with Avocado Dipping Sauce

Prep Time: 20 minutes
Cooking Time: 40 minutes
Servings: 6

Ingredients

For Egg roll Ingredients:
- ¼ cup red pepper, minced
- 12 flour tortillas (7-inch each)
- ½ cup canned black beans (rinsed & drained)
- 2 skinless boneless chicken breasts (approximately 1 pound)
- ¼ cup fresh spinach, minced
- 1 tablespoon dried parsley
- ¼ cup canned jalapeno peppers, diced
- 1 large egg
- ¼ teaspoon cayenne pepper
- 1 teaspoon cumin
- 1 ½ cups Colby jack cheese, shredded
- Cooking oil spray
- ⅔ cup corn, frozen
- 1 teaspoon chili powder
- ¼ cup green onion, minced
- Oil for your deep fryer
- ½ teaspoon salt

For Avocado Ranch Ingredients:
- ¼ teaspoon dried parsley
- 3 teaspoon white vinegar
- ½ cup sour cream
- ¼ teaspoon onion powder
- 1 avocado, fresh
- ½ cup mayonnaise
- 1/8 teaspoon garlic powder
- 1 tablespoon buttermilk
- 1/8 teaspoon dried dill weed
- ¼ teaspoon salt

Directions

1. Lightly coat a large frying pan with the cooking spray and heat it over medium heat. Once hot; add & fry the chicken breasts for a couple of minutes, until cooked through.
2. Add green onions and red peppers to a mini chopper & mince; set aside. Dice & cooked chicken into small bite-sized cubes and then add them to a medium-sized mixing bowl. Add in the black beans and frozen corn to the bowl. Dice the jalapenos, mince the spinach & add them to the bowl as well. Add in the parsley, chili powder, cumin & salt; add the shredded cheese into a small-sized mixing bowl.
3. Generously coat a frying pan with the cooking spray and heat it over medium heat. Add the green onions and peppers; cook until tender, for a minute or two. Add the entire ingredients from the mixing bowl all at once; give everything a good stir until combined well. Cook over medium heat for 5 minutes, stirring every now and then. Add in the cheese & stir until melted and combined well.
4. Now, heat the tortillas in the microwave until hot, for up to 2 minutes and then place a tortilla on a table top or clean counter.
5. Spoon approximately 1/12 of the filling mixture in a line down the middle of the tortilla. Crack an egg into a small-sized bowl & beat well with a whisk. Fold in the sides of your tortilla. Tightly roll the tortilla up, stopping before reaching the end.
6. Using a pastry brush; brush the beaten egg onto the inside of tortilla.
7. Roll the tortilla up the rest of the way.
8. Place the finished egg roll, seam side down on a large-sized cookie sheet.
9. Continue to roll the egg rolls until you have rolled all 12 & placed them onto the cookie sheet. Freeze the egg rolls for 3 hours.
10. Put the entire ingredients including the fresh avocado into a mini chopper. Blend for half a minute, until completely smooth. Transfer to 2 small custard-sized dishes. Cover with a plastic wrap & store in a refrigerator until ready to serve

For Frying:
1. Over moderate heat in a deep fryer; heat the oil until hot. Fry each egg roll for 5 to 7 minutes. Transfer the cooked egg rolls to a plate with some paper towels & let cool.
2. Cut the egg rolls diagonally lengthwise. Serve with the prepared avocado ranch dipping sauce and enjoy.

Chili's Boneless Shanghai Wings

Prep Time: 30 minutes
Cooking Time: 2 hours & 15 minutes
Servings: 4

Ingredients

- 1 cup all-purpose flour
- ¼ cup Louisiana hot sauce
- 1 large egg
- ¼ teaspoon cayenne pepper
- 1 cup milk
- 2 chicken breast fillets
- 1 tablespoon margarine or butter
- ¼ teaspoon paprika
- 4-6 cups vegetable oil
- ½ teaspoon black pepper
- 2 teaspoons salt

Directions

1. Combine flour together with peppers, paprika & salt in a medium-sized bowl. Whisk egg together with milk in a separate small-sized bowl. Slice each chicken breast into 6 pieces. Now, over moderate heat in a deep fryer; heat 4 to 6 cups of vegetable oil until hot.
2. Work in batches, dip chicken pieces first into egg mixture and then into breading blend.
3. When done, arrange them on a plate & let chill for 12 to 15 minutes.
4. Drop each piece carefully into the hot oil & fry until each piece is nicely browned, for 5 to 6 minutes.
5. In the meantime; combine the butter and hot sauce in a small bowl. Microwave the sauce until the butter is just melted, for 20 to 30 seconds; stir until combined well.
6. When you have fried the chicken pieces, remove them to a plate lined with a few paper towels and then place the chicken pieces into a covered container or jar with a lid. Pour the sauce on top of the chicken pieces; cover & gently shake until each piece of chicken is nicely coated with the sauce. Pour the chicken onto a plate; serve the dish with some blue cheese dressing & sliced celery on the side. Enjoy.

Chili's Chicken Crispers

Prep Time: 20 minutes
Cooking Time: 15 minutes
Servings: 4

Ingredients

For Chicken:
- ¾ cup chicken broth
- 10 chicken tenderloins
- ½ cup all-purpose flour
- 1 lightly beaten egg, large
- ¼ cup milk
- 1 cup self-rising flour
- ½ teaspoon black pepper
- 6 to 10 cups vegetable oil or shortening
- 1 ½ teaspoons salt

For Honey Mustard Dressing:
- ¼ teaspoon paprika
- 2 tablespoons Dijon mustard
- ⅔ cup mayonnaise
- ¼ cup honey
- A pinch of cayenne pepper
- 1/8 teaspoon salt

Directions

1. For Sauce: Combine the entire sauce ingredients together in a small bowl. Using a plastic wrap; cover & refrigerate until ready to use.
2. Now, combine egg together with chicken broth, milk, pepper and salt in a medium bowl. Whisk for half a minute. Whisk in the self-rising flour & let sit for a couple of minutes.
3. Place the oil or shortening in a Dutch oven & heat it at 350 F.
4. Place the ½ cup of flour in a medium-sized bowl. Coat each piece of chicken into the flour & then dunk into the batter.
5. Work in batches, carefully lower the battered chicken into the hot oil & fry until turn golden brown, for 7 to 9 minutes.
6. Drain on a paper-towel lined plate or wire rack.

Chili's Chicken Fajita Nachos

Prep Time: 10 minutes
Cooking Time: 45 minutes
Servings: 2

Ingredients

- 1 boneless chicken breast, uncooked; cut into strips
- 16 whole tortilla chips, large (not broken)
- 1 bell pepper; cut in half, deseeded and then sliced into strips
- ½ cup each of Monterey jack cheese & mild cheddar cheese, shredded
- 1 jalapeno, deseeded & cut into slices
- ½ cup of pace thick & chunky salsa
- 1 Vidalia onion; cut in half & sliced
- 2 tablespoons sour cream
- 1 envelope of fajita seasoning mix
- 1 cup shredded lettuce
- 2 tablespoons guacamole

Directions

1. Sauté the chicken together with onion & peppers as mentioned on the Fajita seasoning pack. When done, drain the mixture & set aside.
2. Place the Tortilla Chips on a large, Microwaveable or oven proof plate or platter in a circle. Layer the chicken, peppers & onions over the whole Tortilla chips.
3. Layer the shredded cheeses over the chicken & then top with the Jalapenos.
4. Place the plate inside the oven and cook until the Cheeses are just melted, at 350 F.
5. When the Nachos are ready, add in the shredded Lettuce (in the middle of the platter or plate).
6. Top the Lettuce with the Sour Cream & Salsa (feel free to add Guacamole, if desired). Grab a cold one & Enjoy.

Chili's Cheddar Cheese Bites

Prep Time: 10 minutes
Cooking Time: 10 minutes
Servings: 12

Ingredients

- 1 pound cubed cheddar cheese or cheese curds
- 1 ¼ cups all-purpose flour, divided
- 1 cup beer
- Oil, as required for deep-fat frying

Directions

1. Place ¼ cup of the flour in a large re-sealable plastic bag. Slowly add in the cheese curds & shake until nicely coated.
2. Now, over moderate heat in a deep fryer or an electric skillet; heat the oil. In the meantime, whisk the beer with leftover flour in a large bowl. Slowly dip the cheese curds into the batter & fry until turn golden brown, for 2 to 3 minutes per side. Place them on paper towels to drain.

Chipotle Baba Ghanoush

Prep Time: 10 minutes
Cooking Time: 30 minutes
Servings: 6

Ingredients

- 3 pounds eggplants; sliced in half
- 1 teaspoon garlic, minced
- ¼ teaspoon chipotle powder for dip plus more to sprinkle on top
- 2 tablespoons tahini sesame seed paste
- 1 ½ teaspoon olive oil
- 2 tablespoon lemon juice, freshly squeezed
- 1 teaspoon kosher salt

Directions

1. Preheat your oven to 350F in advance. Place eggplant on a large-sized baking sheet sprayed with non-stick spray or lined with parchment paper, flesh-side down.
2. Bake the eggplants until the flesh is soft, for 30 minutes. Let the eggplants to cool until you can easily handle them. Scrape the meat of the eggplant into a medium-sized bowl; discarding the skins. Add tahini, minced garlic, olive oil, lemon juice, chipotle powder & kosher salt; mix well.
3. Pour into a serving dish & drizzle with more of olive oil & sprinkle some more chipotle powder, if desired. Enjoy.

Chipotle Guacamole

Prep Time: 5 minutes
Cooking Time: 5 minutes
Servings: 4

Ingredients

- 2 Hass avocados halved, large & pitted
- ½ jalapeno pepper including the seeds, finely chopped
- 2 teaspoon lime juice, freshly squeezed
- ¼ cup finely chopped red onion
- 2 tablespoons fresh cilantro leaves, finely chopped
- ¼ teaspoon table salt or kosher salt

Directions

1. Combine avocados with the lime juice in a medium bowl. Toss until coated evenly. Add salt & mash until completely smooth.
2. Stir in the peppers, onion and cilantro. Taste & add more of salt, if required. Serve with some chips on side and enjoy.

Claim Jumper Cheese Potato Cakes

Prep Time: 25 minutes
Cooking Time: 15 minutes
Servings: 6

Ingredients

For Potato Cakes:
- ¼ teaspoon freshly-ground black pepper
- 4 red potatoes, medium (approximately 1 pound) with skins
- ¼ cup cheddar cheese, shredded
- ½ teaspoon fresh cilantro, minced
- ¼ cup Monterey jack cheese, shredded
- 2 tablespoons parmesan cheese, shredded
- ¼ teaspoon garlic powder
- 1 green onion chopped
- ½ teaspoon salt

For Herbed Ranch Salsa:
- ¼ cup tomato, diced & seeded (approximately ½ tomato)
- 2 tablespoons onion, minced
- ½ cup sour cream
- 1 teaspoon minced cilantro, fresh
- ¼ teaspoon ground black pepper
- 1 tablespoon white vinegar
- A pinch of dried dill
- ½ teaspoon salt

For Breading:
- ⅓ cup all-purpose flour
- 1 beaten egg, large
- ⅔ cup breadcrumbs, unseasoned
- 1 cup milk
- ½ teaspoon dried dill
- 2 cups shortening for frying

Directions

1. Boil the potatoes over moderate heat until mostly soft, but still slightly firm, for 25 to 30 minutes. Ensure that you don't overcook them.
2. In the meantime; prepare the herbed ranch salsa by mixing the entire ingredients together in a small bowl. Cover & let this sauce to chill until ready to use.
3. Drain the potatoes & mash in a medium bowl, with the skin on; don't worry if some small chunks of potato remain. Add the leftover ingredients for the potato-cakes & mix well.
4. In a large bowl; combine flour together with breadcrumbs & ½ teaspoon of dill. Combine milk with beaten egg in a separate large-sized bowl. Measure approximately ⅓ cup of the potato mixture into your hands & shape it into a patty approximately the size of a hamburger patty. Drop the potato mixture into the breading mixture, then into the milk and egg and then into the breading again; ensure that the entire surface of the potato-cake is covered with the breading.
5. Arrange them on a plate & repeat the process with the leftover potato mixture. Cover & let the potato-cakes to chill for an hour.
6. Now, over medium to low heat in a large skillet; heat up the shortening (approximately 1 inch). Carefully drop the potato-cakes into the hot oil & fry until golden brown, for 2 to 4 minutes; then place them on paper towels or a rack to drain.
7. Serve the potato-cakes with a bit of herbed ranch salsa poured over the top and enjoy.

Ikea Swedish Meatballs

Prep Time: 30 minutes
Cooking Time: 40 minutes
Servings: 6

Ingredients

- ¾ pound lean ground beef
- 2 tablespoon all-purpose flour
- ½ pound lean ground pork
- 1 cup bread crumbs
- ⅓ white onion, minced
- 2 tablespoon unsalted butter
- ¼ teaspoon ground allspice
- 2 teaspoon kosher salt, or to taste
- ¼ teaspoon white pepper, freshly ground, or to taste
- 1 teaspoon Worcestershire sauce
- ½ cup milk
- 1 teaspoon Worcestershire sauce
- 2 garlic clove, minced
- 1 vegetable oil, for greasing the baking sheet
- 2 tablespoon unsalted butter
- 1 large egg, plus 1 egg white, beaten
- 2 tablespoon fresh parsley, chopped
- 1 ½ cup low sodium beef broth
- Kosher salt & freshly ground black pepper, to taste
- ¼ cup heavy cream

Directions

1. For Meatballs: Put the bread crumbs in a large bowl. Over medium heat in a large skillet; heat 2 tablespoons of the butter until melted.
2. Once done; add onion together with garlic, allspice, ¼ teaspoon of white pepper and 2 teaspoons of salt; cook for 4 to 5 minutes, until soft, stirring frequently.
3. Add milk & 1 teaspoon of the Worcestershire sauce; bring everything together to a simmer. Pour the milk mixture on top of the bread crumbs; stir until you get thick paste like consistency; let cool.
4. Add in the ground pork, ground beef, egg white and egg to the bowl; mix until well combined. Brush a large-sized baking sheet with the vegetable oil. Roll the meat into 1" balls & arrange them on the baking sheet. Using a plastic wrap; cover & let refrigerate for an hour.
5. Preheat your oven to 400 F in advance.
6. Bake the meatballs until cooked through, approximately 20 minutes.
7. For the Gravy: Over moderate heat in a large skillet; heat 2 tablespoons of the butter until melted.
8. Add and cook the flour until smooth, whisking frequently. Whisk in the beef broth & 1 teaspoon of the Worcestershire sauce; bring everything together to a simmer.
9. Add in the meatballs and heavy cream. Decrease the heat to medium low & let simmer for 8 to 10 minutes, until the gravy thickens. Season with black pepper and salt to taste.
10. Transfer to a large-sized serving dish & sprinkle with the fresh parsley. Serve immediately and enjoy.

Cracker Barrel Grilled Chicken Tenders

Prep Time: 5 minutes
Cooking Time: 45 minutes
Servings: 4

Ingredients

- 2 teaspoons lime juice, freshly squeezed
- 1 pound cut chicken breasts or chicken tenders
- 2 tablespoons honey
- ½ cup Italian dressing

Directions

1. Place the chicken tenderloins with wet ingredients into a large plastic bag. Let marinate in a refrigerator for an hour.
2. Add the chicken & liquid to a large skillet. Cook until the liquid is reduced & chicken turns golden, but not dry, over medium heat. Ensure that you turn the chicken pieces a couple of times during the cooking process.

Joe's Crab Shack Great Balls of Fire

Prep Time: 30 minutes
Cooking Time: 30 minutes
Servings: 10

Ingredients

- 4 ounces salad shrimp; minced
- ¼ cup sour cream
- 2 ounces cream cheese
- 1 tablespoon mayonnaise
- 3 jalapenos; minced, seeded
- 1/8 teaspoon chili powder
- 6 ounces crab; canned
- ¼ cup Pepper-jack cheese; shredded
- 4 teaspoons onions; minced
- 1 tablespoon milk
- 2 tablespoons butter
- 1 cup breadcrumbs
- 2 large eggs
- 1 cup oil; for frying
- 1/8 teaspoon paprika
- 1 teaspoon season salt

Directions

1. Combine cream cheese together with butter, mayonnaise & sour cream until blended well. Add in the chili powder, paprika & seasoned salt. Add onion, cheese, jalapenos and green pepper. Add crab & shrimp; mix. Make approximately ¼" balls from the mixture & let refrigerate for half an hour.
2. Beat the eggs with milk. Dip the balls into milk-egg mixture; dredge into the fine bread crumbs. Deep fry in 1 cup of hot oil until turn golden.

Joe's Crab Shack Crab Nacho's

Prep Time: 10 minutes
Cooking Time: 10 minutes
Servings: 3

Ingredients

- 6 ounces crab lump meat
- 1 tablespoon softened butter
- ¼ cup sour cream
- 2 ounces softened cream cheese
- 1/8 teaspoon paprika
- 4 teaspoons yellow onion chopped
- 1 tablespoon green onion, sliced
- ¼ cup shredded mozzarella cheese
- 1 tablespoon mayonnaise
- 4 teaspoons green bell pepper, diced finely
- 1 teaspoon fresh parsley, chopped
- ¼ teaspoon seasoned salt

Directions

1. Mix sour cream together with mayonnaise, cream cheese & butter until completely smooth. Blend in the paprika and seasoned salt. Stir in the crab meat, yellow onions, mozzarella cheese and green pepper.
2. Place in a small shallow baking dish, lightly greased & place in a preheated oven; bake for 12 to 15 minutes, until the mixture starts to bubble, at 350 F.
3. Serve the dip with very lightly salted or unsalted corn chips.

KFC Honey BBQ Wings

Prep Time: 30 minutes
Cooking Time: 30 minutes
Servings: 8

Ingredients

- 20 chicken wings; washed, tips removed & cut in half; shaking off any excess water
- ⅔ cup milk
- 2 cups flour
- 1 bottle barbecue sauce
- 2 large eggs
- Oil, for deep frying
- ¼ cup honey

Directions

1. Combine milk with eggs in a large bowl; mix well & set aside.
2. Mix the barbecue sauce together with honey; mix well & set aside.
3. Put flour in a bag & shake the wings until coated lightly then roll the wings in egg wash; toss them into the flour again. Repeat these steps for a couple of times.
4. Now, over moderate heat in a large saucepan; heat the oil until hot. Work in batches & fry the wings until golden brown, for a couple of minutes per side. Remove and place them on paper towels to drain.
5. Preheat your oven to 325 F in advance. Dip each wing in the barbecue sauce & place them on a cookie sheet, lightly greased (ensure that you don't over-crowd the pieces).
6. Bake until they are no longer shiny, for 15 to 20 minutes.

Hooters Buffalo Wings

Prep Time: 15 minutes
Cooking Time: 25 minutes
Servings: 5

Ingredients

For the Wings:
- ¼ teaspoon paprika
- 10 chicken wing pieces
- ¼ teaspoon cayenne pepper
- s½ cup all-purpose flour
- Vegetable oil, for frying
- ¼ teaspoon salt

For the Sauce:
- ¼ cup butter
- A dash each of garlic powder & pepper
- ¼ cup hot pepper sauce

Directions

1. In a bowl with a lid (large enough to fit the wings); combine the flour together with cayenne pepper, paprika & salt. Place the chicken wings in the bowl; cover with the lid & shake until coated completely & don't stuck together. Place the wings in a refrigerator and let chill for 60 to 90 minutes.
2. Over moderate heat in a deep fryer; heat the oil (enough to cover the wings) until hot.
3. Carefully place the wings into the hot oil & fry until they start to turn dark brown, for 10 to 15 minutes.
4. In the meantime; combine hot pepper sauce together with butter, garlic powder and ground pepper over low heat. Continue to cook until the butter is completely melted & the ingredients are blended well.
5. Remove the wings from fryer & place them on a paper towel to drain. Toss the wings with the sauce in a large bowl until coated evenly. Serve with ranch dressing or bleu cheese, celery and carrots. Enjoy.

Directions

1. Start the process by preparing the dipping sauce in advance. Combine the entire sauce ingredients together in a medium bowl; whisk until combined well. Cover & refrigerate until ready to use.
2. For Chicken: Cut both the chicken breasts down the center lengthwise and make four long strips. Combine egg with the buttermilk in a medium bowl; beat until combined well. Soak the chicken pieces in the egg and buttermilk mixture for 8 to 10 minutes.
3. Line a large-sized baking sheet with an aluminum foil or parchment & coat it lightly with the nonstick cooking spray; set aside & preheat your oven to 375 F in advance.
4. In the meantime, place approximately 2 cups of the Corn Flakes cereal into a large-sized zip-top bag. Seal & crush with a rolling pin until very fine crumbs are formed. Pour the crumbs into a large shallow bowl and then add in the flour, chopped Pecans, black pepper, salt, paprika, granulated garlic and onion powder; mix well. Pour the leftover uncrushed Corn Flakes cereal into a separate large-sized shallow bowl. Remove one of the chicken pieces from the egg and buttermilk mixture; place into the flour mixture; ensure that you coat the pieces well. Dip the chicken piece quickly into the wet mixture again and then roll into the whole cereal flakes; press well. Repeat with the leftover chicken pieces. Arrange the coated pieces onto prepared tray & bake in the preheated oven until cooked through, for 15 to 18 minutes. Remove from oven & serve with the chilled dipping sauce on side. Enjoy.

Houlihan's Shrooms

Prep Time: 5 minutes
Cooking Time: 3 hours & 55 minutes
Servings: 8

Ingredients

For Coating:
- ½ teaspoon cayenne pepper
- 6 -8 button mushrooms, large; cleaned & stems removed, leaving the caps only
- ½ cup milk
- 1 cup flour
- Vegetable oil, as required (for frying)
- 1 ½ teaspoons salt

For Herb Cheese Filling:
- ⅓ cup whipped cream cheese
- ½ teaspoon ranch dressing mix

For Dipping Sauce:
- ¼ teaspoon sugar
- 2 teaspoons Dijon mustard
- ½ cup mayonnaise
- 2 teaspoons prepared horseradish
- ¾ teaspoon vinegar

Directions

1. Combine the cream cheese together with ranch dressing & let sit for 10 to 15 minutes.
2. Once done; fill the mushroom caps with the cheese-herb mixture using a teaspoon.
3. Now, in a small bowl; combine flour together with cayenne pepper and 1 ½ teaspoons of salt; mix well.
4. Pour milk into a separate bowl.
5. Dip each mushroom first into the milk and then into the flour. Do this step for two more times until each mushroom is double-coated.
6. Put the coated mushrooms into the freezer and let for a couple of hours.
7. In the meantime, start preparing the dipping sauce. Combine the entire sauce ingredients together in a small bowl. Cover & let chill until ready to use.
8. Once the mushrooms are frozen, heat the oil (enough to cover the mushrooms) in a deep pot or deep fryer, over moderate heat.
9. Fry the mushrooms until the outside turns a golden brown, for 8 to 10 minutes. Place the mushrooms on paper towels or a rack to drain.
10. Let sit for a few minutes. Serve with some dipping sauce on side and enjoy.

Hard Rock Cafe Tupelo Style Chicken

Prep Time: 20 minutes
Cooking Time: 20 minutes
Servings: 4

Ingredients

For Chicken:
- ½ cup all-purpose flour
- 2 large boneless, skinless chicken breasts
- ¼ teaspoon onion powder
- 1 cup Buttermilk
- ¼ teaspoon black pepper
- 1 large egg
- ¼ teaspoon paprika
- 4 cups corn flakes cereal, divided
- ½ cup pecans, finely chopped
- ¼ teaspoon granulated garlic
- ½ teaspoon salt

For Dipping Sauce:
- 2 tablespoon mayonnaise
- ½ cup prepared Dijon mustard
- 2 teaspoon lime juice, freshly squeezed
- ¼ teaspoon chipotle powder
- 2 tablespoon coarse grain mustard
- ⅛ teaspoon each of black pepper & salt
- 2 tablespoon honey

Hooter's Fried Pickles

Prep Time: 10 minutes
Cooking Time: 30 minutes
Servings: 4

Ingredients

- 1 jar dill pickles (16-oz)
- ½ teaspoon cayenne pepper
- 1 cup all-purpose flour
- ½ teaspoon garlic powder
- 1 large egg
- 4 dashes of hot sauce
- ¼ teaspoon paprika
- 1 cups buttermilk
- Neutral cooking oil such as peanut, vegetable or canola

Directions

1. Over moderate heat in a large pot (8 quart); preheat approximately 2" of oil until hot. Prepare a tray with double paper towel stack and set aside until ready to use.
2. Combine buttermilk together with hot sauce and egg in a medium bowl. Beat with a fork until combined well. Drain the pickle juice from pickle jar & add the pickles to buttermilk mixture; give everything a good stir until combined well.
3. Whisk the flour together with paprika, cayenne pepper and garlic powder in a separate bowl.
4. Add approximately a handful of the pickles to flour mixture; swirl the pickles around & ensure that they are coated well; shaking off any excess flour. Work in batches and drop approximately 7 to 8 of the pickles carefully into the hot oil.
5. Fry the pickles until turn golden brown, for 3 to 5 minutes. Using a large slotted spoon; remove the pickles from oil & place them on a tray lined with paper towels to drain.
6. Serve immediately & enjoy.

Logan's Roadhouse Fried Mushrooms

Prep Time: 10 minutes
Cooking Time: 10 minutes
Servings: 6

Ingredients

- 1 pound white button mushrooms, fresh, small-sized
- 1 ½ teaspoons ground black pepper
- 1 cup all-purpose flour
- 3 cups vegetable oil for frying
- 1 cup buttermilk
- ½ cup water
- 2 teaspoons salt

Directions

1. Fill a deep fryer or large saucepan with approximately 3 to 4" of oil and heat it over moderate heat until hot.
2. Using a damp paper towel; gently clean the mushrooms.
3. Combine flour together with the pepper and salt in a large bowl; stir well until combined well. Combine buttermilk with water in a separate bowl.
4. Dredge the mushrooms first into the seasoned flour; shaking off the excess & then dip them into the buttermilk. Dredge them into the flour again. Knocking off any excess flour from the mushrooms.
5. Gently lower the mushrooms into the hot oil & cook for 2 to 3 minutes, until golden brown. Place them on a wire rack to drain.
6. Serve with your favorite sauce and enjoy.

Lone Star Steakhouse Amarillo Cheese Fries

Prep Time: 10 minutes
Cooking Time: 30 minutes
Servings: 6

Ingredients

- 1 bottle ranch salad dressing (8 ounce)
- 4 strips bacon, cooked, crumbled
- ½ envelope taco seasoning (1.25 ounce)
- 1 package spicy French fries, frozen (32 ounce), prepared as mentioned
- ½ cup Colby jack cheese, shredded

Directions

1. Combine the taco seasoning with ranch dressing; set aside until ready to use.
2. Sprinkle the bacon and cheese evenly over the fries on a large-sized baking sheet. Return the fries to hot oven and bake until the cheese melts.
3. Serve the fries with prepared sauce for dipping and enjoy.

Lavo's "The Meatball"

Prep Time: 2 minutes
Cooking Time: 35 minutes
Servings: 3

Ingredients

- ½ cup Parmigiano Reggiano cheese grated
- 2 pounds ground meatloaf mix (beef, pork and veal)
- ½ cup grated Romano cheese
- 1 cup Italian bread no crust, fresh, cut into 1" cubes
- ½ cup Italian seasoned breadcrumbs, dry
- 3 large eggs
- ½ teaspoon ground black pepper
- 2 tablespoons finely chopped parsley, fresh plus more for garnish
- ¼ cup whole milk
- 2 tablespoons finely chopped basil, fresh
- ½ cup ricotta cheese
- 4 garlic cloves, large, crushed
- ½ cup yellow onion, minced
- 1 cup extra virgin olive oil divided
- 4 cups marinara sauce, bottled or homemade
- 1 teaspoon fine sea salt

Directions

1. Add the fresh Italian bread cubes into the milk and let them soak for 8 to 10 minutes. Squeeze & drain the milk but reserving the bread; set aside until ready to use.
2. Now, over moderate heat in a sauté pan; heat ½ cup of the extra virgin olive oil until hot and then sauté the onions and garlic until soft, for a couple of minutes. Season with black pepper and fine sea salt; set aside to cool down.
3. When garlic and onions are cool, squeeze the excess liquid out & combine them with the meat mixture & the leftover ingredients (except the ricotta cheese, marinara sauce & additional extra-virgin olive oil). Don't over mix.
4. Evenly divide meat mixture into thirds. Making a meatball from each third by tossing from hand to hand.
5. Refrigerate the meatballs for an hour or for overnight.
6. Now, brown the meatballs in the leftover ½ extra virgin olive oil in an oven-safe sauté pan, over moderate heat; rolling so all sides are nicely browned. Remove from skillet and place them on a large plate lined with paper towel; discard the extra oil and fat. Clean the skillet & add the meatballs back to it.
7. Preheat your oven to 350 F. Cover the meatballs with marinara sauce. Bring the skillet to a boil again & then immediately transfer to the hot oven. Continue baking until the middle of the meatballs reflects 160 F, for an hour.
8. Let cool for 10 to 15 minutes before serving. Serve topped with ricotta cheese & freshly chopped parsley. Enjoy.

Longhorn Steakhouse Parmesan Encrusted Asparagus

Prep Time: 10 minutes
Cooking Time: 10 minutes
Servings: 6

Ingredients

- 1 pound asparagus, bottoms trimmed
- 2 cup buttermilk
- ½ cup parmesan, grated
- 10 gram parmesan shaving
- 1 ½ cup flour
- 2 cups olive oil
- 1 teaspoon seasoned salt

Directions

1. Combine flour together with parmesan & seasoned salt in a large bowl.
2. Add the asparagus into the flour mixture; coat them well and then dip them into the buttermilk & dredge them into the flour again.
3. Over moderate heat in a large frying pan, heat the oil until hot & carefully add and fry the asparagus until both sides turn golden brown.
4. Just before serving; garnish your recipe with the parmesan shavings; serve warm & enjoy.

Margaritaville Volcano Nachos

Prep Time: 30 minutes
Cooking Time: 30 minutes
Servings: 10

Ingredients

- Diced Tomato
- 1 bag tortilla chips
- Canned jalapeno slices
- Guacamole (store bought or fresh)
- 1 - 2 cans of chili or homemade
- Cheddar cheese & Monterey Jack cheese, shredded
- 1 jar salsa con queso
- Green Onion
- Sour Cream

Directions

1. Preheat your oven to 375 F in advance.
2. Meanwhile, prepare the nachos.
3. Cover the bottom of an oven safe dish with a layer of tortilla chips.
4. Now add in the salsa con queso and add chili to the top layer or adding the chili on all layers.
5. Sprinkle with the shredded cheeses & repeat these steps for two more times
6. Once you have assembled your Volcano, place it in the preheated oven until the cheese is completely melted or for 7 to 10 minutes.
7. Remove from oven & top with green onions, tomatoes, guacamole, jalapenos & sour cream. Serve and enjoy.

Longhorn Steakhouse Firecracker Chicken

Prep Time: 15 minutes
Cooking Time: 45 minutes
Servings: 8

Ingredients

For Firecracker Chicken:
- 2-3 pounds chicken breasts, boneless, marinated, grilled and shredded

For Avocado Lime Sauce:
- Juice of 3 to 4 limes, medium-sized
- 1 avocado
- Ranch dressing, optional
- 1-2 garlic cloves, pressed or finely minced
- Olive oil, as required
- Salt to taste

For Firecracker Sauce:
- 6 flour tortillas (6" size)
- 1 cup Louisiana hot sauce
- ¾ teaspoon granulated sugar
- 2 teaspoons cornstarch
- 1 teaspoon garlic powder
- 5 tablespoons butter
- 1 ½ to 2 cups pepper jack cheese, shredded
- 2 tablespoons water
- ½ teaspoon ground cayenne pepper

For Firecracker Marinade:
- 1 tablespoon apple cider vinegar
- ½ cup Louisiana hot sauce
- 1 teaspoon sea salt or kosher salt
- 1 teaspoon granulated sugar

Directions

For Firecracker Chicken:
1. Combine the entire marinade ingredients together in a large bowl; give them a good stir until the salt is completely dissolved. Pour the mixture into a large-sized zip top freezer bag & then add in the chicken pieces. Turn several times until the chicken pieces are evenly coated with the marinade.
2. Place marinate in refrigerator for 2 hours; turning every now and then to ensure that the chicken is coated evenly with the marinade. After the chicken breasts have marinated; roast or grill them then shred the cooked chicken. Place the shredded chicken into a plastic container with a lid. Pour a generous quantity of the sauce on top; cover & gently toss or stir the wings to coat the chicken with the sauce.
3. In same container mix in cheese with the chicken. Gently toss to coat well and then wrap the tortillas in a moist cloth; microwave until hot or for 1 ½ minutes, on high temperature. Spoon approximately 1/6 of the mixture into the middle of a tortilla. Fold in the ends & then roll the tortilla over the mixture. Tightly roll the tortilla and then pierce with a toothpick to hold together. Arrange the wraps on a plate; cover with a plastic wrap & freeze for 4 hours or overnight.

For Eggrolls:
1. Heat 6 cups oil until hot. Deep fry the wraps oil for 12 to 15 minutes; remove to a rack or paper towels to drain. Carefully remove the toothpicks. Slice each eggroll diagonally lengthwise & arrange them on a plate covered with lettuce leaves around a small bowl of the ranch dressing or avocado dipping sauce. Garnish with the chopped tomato.

For Firecracker Sauce:
1. Combine sauce ingredients with water & cornstarch over medium heat in a small saucepan until it starts boiling. Decrease the heat & let simmer for 5 minutes. Combine the cornstarch with 2 tablespoons of water; stir until no lumps remain. Stir into the mixture in sauce pan & continue to heat over medium high heat until the sauce thickens. Immediately remove the pan from heat; set aside to cool.

For Avocado Lime Sauce:
1. Mash the avocado and then combine the lime juice, add a dash of olive oil, garlic & salt. Whisk together until completely smooth.

Margaritaville Jamaica Mistica Wings

Prep Time: 10 minutes
Cooking Time: 2 hours & 10 minutes
Servings: 4

Ingredients

- 10 chicken wings
- 4 -8 cups vegetable oil

For Mango Ranch Dipping Sauce:
- ¼ cup mango juice, fresh
- 1 bottle Hidden Valley Original Ranch Dressing (8 ounce)
- ½ jalapeno, minced
- Pepper & salt to taste

For Honey Habanero Sauce:
- ¼ teaspoon garlic powder
- 1 can tomato paste (6 ounce)
- ½ cup Worcestershire sauce
- 1/8 teaspoon hickory liquid smoke
- ¼ cup honey
- ½ teaspoon dried parsley
- ¼ cup molasses
- 1 habanero pepper, minced
- ½ teaspoon dried onion flakes
- 1 teaspoon red pepper flakes, crushed
- ½ teaspoon onion powder
- 1 teaspoon ground black pepper
- ½ teaspoon chili powder
- 1 cup water
- ⅓ cup white vinegar

Directions

1. For Habanero Honey sauce: Over moderate heat in a large saucepan; combine the entire sauce ingredients (except the vinegar) together. Bring everything together to a boil and then decrease the heat; let the sauce to simmer until sauce reduces by about half and thickens, for an hour, uncovered. Immediately remove the sauce from heat and then add in the vinegar; cover until ready to use.
2. Now, prepare the mango ranch dipping sauce by mixing the ingredients together in a small-sized bowl. Cover & let chill until ready to use.
3. Now, over moderate heat in a deep fryer; heat 4 to 8 cups of oil until hot.
4. Carefully drop the wings into the hot oil & until turn golden brown, fry for 8 to 12 minutes. Place them on paper towels for a couple of minutes to drain. Sprinkle with pepper and salt to taste.
5. Put the wings in a large metal or glass bowl and then add ½ cup of the prepared habanero honey sauce; toss until the wings are coated well. Serve with some dipping sauce on side and enjoy.

Noodles and Company Spicy Asian Meatballs

Prep Time: 15 minutes
Cooking Time: 1 hour & 5 minutes
Servings: 5 dozen

Ingredients

- 2 pounds ground pork
- ½ medium onion, chopped finely
- 1 lightly beaten egg, large
- ⅔ cup Japanese panko bread crumbs
- 1 tablespoon fresh gingerroot, minced
- 3 tablespoons fresh cilantro, minced
- 1 jalapeno pepper, seeded & finely chopped
- 3 tablespoons soy sauce, reduced-sodium
- ⅓ cup water chestnuts, sliced, minced
- 4 garlic cloves, minced

For the Sauce:
- 2 tablespoons chicken broth
- 1 tablespoon soy sauce, reduced-sodium
- 2 cups sweet & sour sauce
- 1 ½ teaspoons fresh gingerroot, minced
- ¼ cup duck sauce
- 1 tablespoon fresh cilantro, minced
- ¼ cup barbecue sauce
- 2 garlic cloves, minced
- Green onions, thinly sliced, optional

Directions

1. Preheat your oven to 375 F in advance. Combine egg together with onion, water chestnuts, cilantro, jalapeno pepper, soy sauce, garlic cloves & gingerroot in a large bowl; mix well & then stir in the bread crumbs. Add in the pork; thoroughly mix and make approximately 1 ¼" balls from the mixture. Place the meatballs on a lightly greased rack in a 15x10x1-in. baking pan and bake in the preheated oven until browned lightly, for 18 to 22 minutes.
2. Transfer the meatballs to a slow cooker, 4-quarts. Mix the entire sauce ingredients (except the optional ingredient) in a small bowl. Pour on top of the cooked meatballs. Cover & cook until the meatballs are cooked through, for 3 to 4 hours on low heat. Sprinkle with the green onions, if desired. Serve and enjoy.

McMenamins Cajun Tots

Prep Time: 5 minutes
Cooking Time: 40 minutes
Servings: 6

Ingredients

- 2 pounds tater tots, frozen (1 bag)
- ¾ teaspoon cayenne pepper
- 6 tablespoon unsalted butter
- ½ teaspoon onion powder
- 1 teaspoon garlic powder
- 5 teaspoon Cajun seasoning
- 1 teaspoon rosemary
- 2 tablespoon vegetable oil
- 1 teaspoon black pepper
- ½ teaspoon salt

Directions

1. Preheat your oven to the temperature mentioned on the bag of your tater tots.
2. Pour butter and oil into a high-sided sauté pan or small pot; heat it over medium heat, give them a good stir until it just begins to boil and combines well.
3. In the meantime, combine the entire spices together in a small bowl; stirring frequently.
4. Remove the butter-oil mixture from the heat & add in the spices, stirring frequently until combined well.
5. Add the frozen tots to large-sized bowl & evenly drizzle with the butter - oil -spices mixture.
6. Tightly cover the bowl with a plastic wrap & toss gently until all tots are evenly coated.
7. Evenly spread the tots on a large baking sheet in a single layer & cook as per the directions mentioned on the bag until very crispy. Serve hot & enjoy.

Panda Express Cream Cheese Wontons

Prep Time: 15 minutes
Cooking Time: 10 minutes
Servings: 24

Ingredients

- 24 wonton wrappers
- 8 ounces cream cheese, softened
- 1/8 teaspoon garlic powder
- 2 tablespoons scallions, minced
- Oil, as required

Directions

1. Combine the cream cheese together with scallions and garlic powder together in a small bowl.
2. Preheat a couple inches of oil over moderate heat in a heavy bottomed pot until hot.
3. Put 1 tablespoon of the prepared mixture into the middle of a wonton wrapper & add water to the edges with your finger.
4. Push the four centers of each side into the center; pressing them together to seal.
5. Once the center is connected from all four sides connect the little wings coming out from the middle
6. Prepare the entire wontons like this.
7. Cook in the hot oil until turn golden brown. Serve and enjoy.

Panera Bread Broccoli Cheese Soup

Prep Time: 15 minutes
Cooking Time: 55 minutes
Servings: 8

Ingredients

- 1 tablespoon butter
- 1 ½ cups broccoli florets, coarsely chopped
- ½ onion, chopped
- 2 ½ cups sharp Cheddar cheese, shredded
- ¼ cup flour
- 2 cups milk
- 1 stalk celery, sliced thinly
- 2 cups chicken stock
- 1 cup carrots, matchstick-cut
- ¼ cup melted butter
- Ground black pepper & salt to taste

Directions

1. Over medium-high heat in a large skillet; heat 1 tablespoon of the butter until completely melted. Once done; add & sauté the onion for 3 to 5 minutes, until translucent; set aside.
2. Whisk in ¼ cup of the melted butter & flour together over medium-low heat in a large saucepan; cook for 3 to 4 minutes, until the flour loses its granular texture; feel free to add a few tablespoons of milk, if required to prevent the flour from burning.
3. Slowly pour milk into the flour mixture; continue to whisk. Stir the chicken stock into the milk mixture. Bring everything together to a simmer; cook for 15 to 20 more minutes, until the mixture is thickened & flour taste is gone. Add broccoli together with the carrots, celery & sautéed onion; let everything to simmer for 20 minutes, until the vegetables are very tender.
4. Stir the Cheddar cheese into the vegetable mixture until the cheese melts completely and then Season with pepper and salt to taste.

PF Chang's Bang Bang Shrimp

Prep Time: 15 minutes
Cooking Time: 30 minutes
Servings: 6 persons

Ingredients

- ½ pound shrimp, medium, peeled & deveined
- 2 tablespoon Sriracha sauce
- ½ cup all-purpose flour
- 1 teaspoon soy sauce
- ½ cup corn-starch
- 1 large egg
- ⅓ cup sweet chili sauce
- Green Onion, sliced, for garnish
- ½ cup mayonnaise
- 1 teaspoon Salt

Directions

1. Combine Sriracha sauce together with sweet chili sauce and mayonnaise in a small-sized bowl; mix well
2. Taste & adjust the amount of seasoning, if required; set aside until ready to use.
3. Place the peeled & deveined shrimp into a medium-sized bowl.
4. Add in the egg and soy sauce; mix until combined well; set aside.
5. Add flour together with corn starch & salt in a separate medium - sized bowl; mix well.
6. Slowly add shrimps to the flour mixture using a fork or chop sticks. Only add a few at a time.
7. Generously coat the shrimp with the flour mixture using a spoon.
8. Shake off any excess flour & place the shrimps on a large plate. Repeat this step until all shrimp are nicely coated with the flour mixture.
9. Now, over moderate heat in a large skillet; heat the oil until hot.
10. Carefully add the coated shrimps to the hot oil; don't crowd them.
11. Cook for a minute.. Flip & cook the other side for 2 more minutes.
12. Remove from oil to a large bowl and pour in the reserved chili-mayonnaise sauce mixture. Gently mix until nicely coated. Serve immediately & enjoy.

PF Chang's Chicken Lettuce Wraps

Prep Time: 10 minutes
Cooking Time: 20 minutes
Servings: 4

Ingredients

- 1 tablespoon olive oil
- 1 pound ground chicken
- 2 cloves garlic minced
- 1 onion finely diced
- ¼ cup hoisin sauce
- 2 tablespoons soy sauce
- 1 tablespoon rice wine vinegar
- 1 tablespoon freshly grated ginger
- ½ teaspoon sesame oil
- 1 teaspoon sugar
- 1 tablespoon Sriracha Optional
- 8 ounces whole water chestnuts drained and diced
- 2 green onions thinly sliced
- Salt and pepper to taste
- 1 head butter lettuce

Directions

1. Over medium-high heat in a large skillet; heat the olive oil until hot. Add and cook the chicken for 5 minutes, until browned & cooked through; as you cook the chicken, don't forget to crumble it.
2. Stir in the sesame oil, onions, garlic, hoisin sauce, ginger, rice wine vinegar, soy sauce, Sriracha and sugar. Continue to cook for a couple of minutes, until onions are soft & translucent, stirring occasionally.
3. Stir in the sliced green onions and chestnuts, pepper and salt; continue to cook for a minute more. Spoon approximately 3 to 4 tablespoons into the middle of each lettuce leaf; serve immediately & enjoy.

PF Chang's Hunan Dragon Wings

Prep Time: 30 minutes
Cooking Time: 30 minutes
Servings: 2 persons

Ingredients

- 2 chicken breast fillets

For Sauce
- 3 to 4 garlic cloves, chopped (approximately 2 tablespoon)
- 2 tablespoon white distilled vinegar
- 3 green onions, chopped (approximately 3 tablespoons)
- 1 cup pineapple juice
- 4 teaspoon granulated sugar
- 1 teaspoon soy sauce
- 2 tablespoon chili sauce
- 1 cup plus 2 teaspoon vegetable oil
- 2 tablespoon water
- ⅓ cup plus ½ teaspoon cornstarch

Directions

1. Over moderate heat in a medium saucepan; heat 2 teaspoons of the vegetable oil until hot. Once done; add & sauté the onion and garlic for just a couple of seconds; keep an eye on everything, don't let it burn, then quickly add in the pineapple juice, followed by the vinegar, chili sauce, soy sauce and sugar.
2. Dissolve cornstarch in approximately 2 tablespoons of water & add it to the saucepan. Bring everything together to a boil & continue to simmer until thick & syrupy, for 3 to 5 minutes.
3. Over medium heat in a medium saucepan; heat 1 cup of oil until hot. Chop the chicken breast fillets into small bite-size pieces. Toss the chicken pieces with cornstarch in a medium bowl until well-dusted.
4. Add & sauté the coated chicken in the hot oil for a couple of minutes, until turn light brown, stirring occasionally. Remove the chicken to paper towels or a rack to drain. Pour the chicken into a medium-sized bowl and add sauce; toss well until the chicken is nicely coated. Serve immediately with some rice on the side & enjoy.

PF Chang's Spare Ribs

Prep Time: 15 minutes
Cooking Time: 2 hours & 40 minutes
Servings: 6 persons

Ingredients

- 1 rack pork spareribs
- 1 tablespoon white vinegar
- ½ cup Hoisin-sauce
- 1 teaspoon sesame seeds
- ⅓ cup light brown sugar, packed
- 1 tablespoon green onion, diced
- 2 tablespoon onions, minced
- 1 cup light corn syrup
- ½ cup water
- 1 cup ketchup

Directions

1. Preheat your oven to 300 F in advance.
2. Combining the entire sauce ingredients together over medium heat in a medium-sized saucepan. Bring the mixture to a boil and then decrease the heat; let simmer until thick, for 5 minutes. Set aside at room temperature & let cool.
3. Lightly season the ribs & then brush both sides with the prepared sauce. Lay the ribs, meaty side down and shiny side out on two layers of foil. Lay two layers of foil on top & tightly roll and crimp the edges, edges facing up to seal.
4. Arrange them on the baking sheet & bake in the preheated oven until the meat is starting to shrink away from the ends of the bone, for 2 to 2 ½ hours. Immediately remove from the oven and heat the broiler. Cut the ribs into serving sized portions of 2 or 3 ribs. Arrange them on broiler pan, bony side up.
5. Brush with the sauce & broil until the sauce is cooked on & bubbly, for a minute or two. Turn the ribs over & repeat this step with the other side. Just before serving; coat the ribs with more of sauce.

PF Chang's Spicy Green Beans

Prep Time: 10 minutes
Cooking Time: 1 hour & 10 minutes
Servings: 8 persons

Ingredients

- ¾ pound green beans, fresh
- 1 ½ tablespoon garlic, minced
- 1 tablespoon sesame oil
- Red pepper, crushed to taste

For the Sauce:
- 1 tablespoon garlic-chili sauce
- 1 teaspoon green onions, chopped
- ½ teaspoon sugar
- 1 teaspoon rice vinegar
- 1 tablespoon soy sauce, gluten-free

Directions

1. Wash & trim the green beans, then cut them into fairly even pieces. Mix the green onions together with chili garlic sauce, soy sauce, rice vinegar & sugar in a separate bowl.
2. Heat the sesame oil in a wok or large pan, over medium-high heat and then add in the garlic. Sauté for 30 seconds and then add in the crushed red pepper and green beans. Cook until the beans turn bright green, for 3 to 4 minutes, stirring often. Stir in the sauce & cook until just heated through. Serve warm & enjoy.

PF Chang's Crispy Green Beans

Prep Time: 10 minutes
Cooking Time: 30 minutes
Servings: 4

Ingredients

- 1 pound green beans
- Vegetable oil, for frying
- ½ teaspoon ground black pepper, plus more for seasoning
- 2 teaspoon salt, plus more for seasoning

For the Dipping Sauce:
- 6 green onions, chopped coarsely (only whites)
- 1 cup vegan mayonnaise or 1 cup mayonnaise
- 4 garlic cloves, chopped coarsely
- ½ teaspoon prepared horseradish
- 2 ½ tablespoon Sriracha sauce

For the Batter:
- 1 cup all-purpose flour
- 1 cup beer

Directions

1. Preheat your oil to 375 F in advance. Combine the entire batter ingredients together in a medium-sized bowl.
2. Dip the green beans into the batter to coat using a fork; letting any excess batter to drip off. Work in batches & fry in the hot oil until golden & crisp. Remove from oil to a sheet tray lined with paper towel. Sprinkle with pepper and salt to taste.
3. Combine the entire sauce ingredients together in a blender. Serve with the fried green beans and enjoy.

PF Chang's Dynamite Shrimp

Prep Time: 15 minutes
Cooking Time: 15 minutes
Servings: 6

Ingredients

- 15 to 20 shrimps, large, peeled & deveined
- Vegetable oil for frying

For the Batter:
- 4 tablespoon corn flour
- 1 large egg
- ¼ teaspoon each of black pepper & salt

For the Sauce:
- 5 tablespoon hot sauce
- 1 teaspoon light honey
- ½ cup mayonnaise
- 1 teaspoon rice vinegar
- 3 tablespoon tomato ketchup
- 1 garlic clove, minced
- ¼ teaspoon chili powder or paprika
- 1 teaspoon sesame oil

For Garnishing:
- Spring onion, sliced

Directions

1. Drain the shrimps & mix them with the entire batter ingredients. Now, over moderate heat in a large frying pan; heat the oil until hot & fry the shrimps for 30 seconds (ensure that shrimps are immersed completely in the hot oil). Immediately remove & place them on a kitchen tissue to drain.
2. Combine the entire sauce ingredients together in a large bowl until blended well. Transfer it into a cocktail glass or pudding bowl. Toss the fried shrimps into it & mix well using a large spoon. Serve garnished with the spring onions and enjoy.

Red Lobster Parrot Bay Coconut Shrimp

Prep Time: 45 minutes
Cooking Time: 25 minutes
Servings: 4 persons

Ingredients

- 1 ½ cups all-purpose flour
- 2 tablespoons granulated sugar
- ½ cup sour cream
- 7 cups canola oil
- ¼ cup canned pineapple, crushed
- 12 large shrimp, peeled and deveined (roughly ½ pound)
- ½ cup flaked coconut
- 2 tablespoons granulated sugar
- ¼ cup pina colada nonalcoholic drink mix
- 1 cup panko Japanese-style bread crumbs
- 2 tablespoons coconut rum
- 1 cup milk
- ¼ teaspoon salt
- Salsa

Directions

1. Prepare the pina colada dipping sauce by combining sour cream together with crushed pineapple, pina colada nonalcoholic drink mix & granulated sugar.
2. Using a plastic wrap; cover & let chill in a fridge until ready to use.
3. Now, over moderate heat in a large pan; heat the oil until hot.
4. Measure approximately ¾ cup of the flour into a medium-sized bowl.
5. Combine the leftover flour together with sugar & salt in a separate medium-sized bowl.
6. Stir rum and milk into the flour mixture. Let the batter to stand for 5 minutes.
7. In the meantime, combine the shredded coconut together with panko breadcrumbs into a third medium-sized bowl.
8. Butterfly cut each shrimp before you start the battering: Slice through the top of the shrimp using a sharp knife; spreading the shrimp open and leaving the tail intact. To batter the shrimp, dip each one into the flour and then into the wet batter; coat each shrimp with the coconut-panko mixture.
9. Arrange the shrimp pieces on a large plate until all of them are nicely battered. Work in batches & fry the shrimp in the hot oil until golden brown, for 2 to 3 minutes.
10. Remove the shrimp to paper towels or a rack to drain. Serve the shrimp with pina colada dipping sauce on side, along with your favorite salsa or a small dish and enjoy.

Red Lobster Bacon-Wrapped Stuffed Shrimp

Prep Time: 15 minutes
Cooking Time: 35 minutes
Servings: 2 persons

Ingredients

- 5 pieces bacon, thinly sliced
- 5 shrimp, large

For Dipping Sauce
- 1 ounce Monterey jack pepper cheese
- 1/3 cup ranch dressing
- 3 slices of jalapenos, fresh
- 1/4 teaspoon dried cilantro

For Seasoning:
- 1/4 teaspoon paprika
- A dash each of allspice, fresh ground pepper & cayenne pepper
- 1/4 teaspoon salt

Directions

1. Preheat your oven to broil.
2. Combine the entire seasoning ingredients together in a small bowl and prepare the seasoning blend; set aside until ready to use.
3. Now, combine the cilantro with ranch dressing in a medium bowl and prepare the dipping sauce.
4. Over medium-high heat in a large frying pan; cook the bacon for 2 to 3 minutes per side; ensure that it's not crispy or brown.
5. When done; place the bacon slices on paper towels to drain.
6. Shell the shrimp, leaving the tail & last segment of the shell.
7. Remove the dark vein from the back & then cut down into the back of the shrimp, without cutting all the way through, so that the shrimp is nearly butter flied open.
8. Fill a small bowl with a cup of water. Add in the shrimp & jalapeño peppers; microwave for 60 to 90 seconds, on high power.
9. Immediately remove the water from the bowl and then remove the jalapeño slices as well; pour a cup of cold water over the shrimp.
10. Place the jalapeño pepper slices and shrimp on paper towels to drain.
11. Cut the jalapeño slices in half; removing the seeds.
12. Place one slice into the slit on the back of a shrimp.
13. Cut an inch-long chunk of cheese (roughly ¼" thick) & then place it over the slice of jalapeño.
14. Wrap a piece of bacon around the shrimp, beginning where the cheese is.
15. Start wrapping the thinnest end of the bacon.
16. Go 1 ½ times around the shrimp & then cut off the excess bacon and slide a skewer through the shrimp, starting with the end where the cheese is and piercing the cut end of the bacon on the other side.
17. Repeat with the remaining shrimp and slide them onto the skewer with the tails facing the same direction.
18. Put the skewer onto a broiler pan or baking sheet and sprinkle a coating of the seasoning blend (very light) over the shrimp; broil in the preheated oven until the cheese begins to ooze and the bacon starts to turn brown, for 3 to 4 minutes.
19. Serve over a bed of rice, if desired and enjoy.

Red Lobster Cheddar Bay Crab Bake

Prep Time: 10 minutes
Cooking Time: 15 minutes
Servings: 11 persons

Ingredients

- 1 tablespoon sugar
- 2 cups all-purpose flour
- 1 cup buttermilk
- 2 teaspoons garlic powder
- 1 tablespoon baking powder
- ½ cup melted unsalted butter
- 2 cups cheddar cheese, shredded
- ¾ teaspoon salt

For Garlic Butter Topping:
- 3 tablespoon melted unsalted butter
- 1 tablespoon fresh parsley, chopped finely
- ½ teaspoon garlic powder

Directions

1. Line a large-sized baking sheet with the parchment paper; set aside and preheat your oven to 450 F in advance.
2. Combine flour together with garlic powder, sugar & salt in a large-sized mixing bowl.
3. Whisk the buttermilk together with the melted butter. Combine the mixture with the dry ingredients; continue to mix until well incorporated and then fold in the cheddar cheese.
4. Measure out each biscuit in a ¼ cup measuring cup; spooning the dough out onto the prepared baking sheet.
5. Bake in the preheated oven until turn golden brown, for 10 to 12 minutes.
6. Combine the entire garlic butter topping ingredients together in a large bowl & brush onto each biscuit.

Red Lobster Seafood Stuffed Mushrooms

Prep Time: 15 minutes
Cooking Time: 20 minutes
Servings: 4 servings

Ingredients

- 1 pound mushrooms, fresh, wiped clean & stems removed
- ½ pound imitation crab meat
- 2 cups crushed oyster crackers
- 1 tablespoon butter
- ¼ cup each of onion, celery & red pepper, finely diced
- 4 garlic cloves, minced
- ½ cup cheddar cheese, shredded
- 1 large egg
- ½ tablespoon garlic powder
- 6 slices provolone cheese
- 1 tablespoon oil
- ½ cup water
- 1 teaspoon each of Old bay, pepper & salt

Directions

1. Preheat butter and oil over moderate heat in a medium sized skillet. Once done; add & sauté the celery together with red pepper and onion for a couple of minutes, until soft and then add in the garlic.
2. Chop half of the mushroom stems & mix them together with the leftover ingredients (except the provolone cheese). Add in the cooked vegetables.
3. Stuff the mixture into the mushrooms & place ¼ slice of cheese over the top.
4. Bake for 10 to 15 minutes at 400 F. Serve immediately and enjoy.

Red Robbin No-fire Peppers

Prep Time: 10 minutes
Cooking Time: 30 minutes
Servings: 4

Ingredients

- Hot pepper jelly
- Sour cream
- 1 ds Paprika
- ¼ pound Cream cheese
- 1/8 teaspoon Garlic powder
- 1 teaspoon onion powder
- 1/2 cup Cornflake crumbs
- 3/4 teaspoon Salt
- 1 teaspoon Vegetable oil
- 4 large jalapeno peppers ; Fresh
- ⅔ cup Self-rising flour
- Vegetable oil ; for frying
- 2 Eggs

Directions

1. Remove the stems from jalapenos and then slice each one down the middle lengthwise; removing the inner membranes and seeds.
2. Wash your hands and then poach the jalapenos halves in a saucepan half-filled with boiling water until tender, for 10 to 15 minutes. Drain well & set aside until cool enough to handle
3. Blot with a paper towel or cloth to dry the inside of each jalapeno slice, then spread approximately ½ ounce of the cream cheese into each jalapenos half using a teaspoon.
4. Beat the eggs in a small-sized shallow bowl and then add oil & ¼ teaspoon of salt; whisk well.
5. Combine flour together with onion powder, paprika, garlic powder and ½ teaspoon salt in a separate shallow bowl; adding the cornflake crumbs into a third medium-sized shallow bowl.
6. Work in batches and slowly dip each stuffed jalapeno first into the egg mixture, then into the flour mixture. Repeat this step and dip the jalapeno again into the egg & then into the flour. Finally, dip the jalapeno back into the egg, then into the cornflake crumbs.
7. Put the coated peppers side by side on a plate & into the freezer for a couple of hours.
8. When the peppers are frozen, heat the vegetable oil (enough to cover the jalapenos) to approximately 350 F in a deep saucepan or deep fryer. Fry the peppers until the outside turns golden brown, for 3 ½ to 4 minutes. Place them on paper towels or a rack to drain. Serve hot with some sour cream and pepper jelly on the side.

Ruth's Chris Barbecued Shrimp

Prep Time: 15 minutes
Cooking Time: 40 minutes
Servings: 4 persons

Ingredients

For Shrimp & Sauce:
- 20 large shrimp, peeled & deveined, tails left on
- 2 tablespoon butter
- ¼ cup white wine
- 2 tablespoon Worcestershire Sauce
- ¼ teaspoon cayenne
- 4 ounces butter
- ½ teaspoon Tabasco sauce
- 3 tablespoon green onions, chopped plus more cut on the bias for garnish
- ¼ teaspoon paprika
- 2 teaspoon garlic, chopped
- Salt to taste

For Roasted Garlic Mashed Potatoes
- 2 potatoes, medium to large- sized
- 1 large garlic clove, roasted
- 2 tablespoon butter
- ¼ cup milk
- Salt to taste

Directions

1. Boil & mash the potatoes. Add in the milk, butter, garlic & salt; set aside until ready to use but keep it warm all the time.
2. Now, over medium-high heat in a large cast iron pan; heat 2 tablespoon of butter until completely melted and hot. Carefully add & cook the shrimp until just done, stirring every now and then (if required, work in batches but ensure that you don't over-crowd them). Remove the shrimp & set aside.
3. Cook the green onions in the leftover butter for a minute and then add in the wine; let simmer until decreased by half. Decrease the heat to low & then add in the garlic, Tabasco, Worcestershire, paprika, cayenne pepper & salt. Cook for a minute or two more. Slowly add in the butter cubes & stir after each addition. Add the shrimp again; toss heat through & to coat. Serve with roasted garlic mashed potatoes and enjoy.

Ruby Tuesday Thai Phoon Shrimp

Prep Time: 5 minutes
Cooking Time: 35 minutes
Servings: 6 persons

Ingredients

For Shrimp:
- 30 shrimp, medium, peeled & de-veined
- ¼ teaspoon garlic powder
- 1 beaten egg, large
- ½ teaspoon ground black pepper
- 1 cup all-purpose flour
- ¼ teaspoon ground cayenne pepper
- 1 teaspoon salt
- ¾ teaspoon baking soda
- 1 cup milk
- ¼ teaspoon onion powder
- Vegetable oil, for deep frying

For Sauce:
- 1/8 teaspoon ground paprika
- 4 teaspoons Asian chili garlic sauce
- ¼ teaspoon ground cayenne pepper
- 2 teaspoons granulated sugar
- ½ cup mayonnaise

Directions

1. For Sauce: Combine the entire chili sauce ingredients together in a small bowl until combined well.
2. For Shrimp: Combine the beaten egg together with milk in a large-sized shallow bowl. Combine with baking soda, cayenne pepper, garlic powder, onion powder, black pepper and salt. Coat each shrimp first with the flour and then dip the floured shrimp into the egg & milk mixture and then into the flour again. Arrange the coated shrimp on a plate & pop them in a fridge for 10 minutes. Over moderate heat in a large pan; heat the oil until hot; work in batches and fry the shrimps until golden brown or for 3 to 4 minutes, approximately 8 to 10 shrimps at a time.
3. Spoon approximately ¼ cup of the sauce on top of the shrimp; gently stir the shrimp until coated with the sauce. Serve immediately with the leftover chili sauce on side and enjoy.

Outback Steakhouse Alice Springs Quesadilla

Prep Time: 10 minutes
Cooking Time: 40 minutes
Servings: 6 persons

Ingredients

- 4 -6 boneless skinless chicken breasts
- 1 cup honey
- 2 tablespoons butter
- 1 teaspoon lemon juice, freshly squeezed
- 2 cups mushrooms, sliced
- 1 cup Dijon mustard
- 12 pre-cooked slices of bacon
- Tortilla
- 1 tablespoon canola oil
- 3 cups Mexican blend cheese, shredded
- ½ teaspoon pepper
- 1 tablespoon vegetable oil
- ½ teaspoon salt

Directions

1. Combine mustard together with honey, 1 tablespoon of oil & lemon juice using an electric mixer for a minute.
2. Pour approximately ½ of the mixture on top of the chicken in a gallon-sized zip-lock bag and let marinate in a fridge for a couple of hours.
3. Chill the leftover marinade with chicken to serve.
4. After marinating the chicken, put the leftover oil in a frying pan & sear the chicken on both sides for a couple of minutes per side, until cooked through, over moderate heat.
5. Transfer the cooked chicken to a pan & brush with the marinade; keep warm.
6. In the meantime; heat the butter in a large frying pan & sauté the mushrooms. Remove from heat.
7. Cut the chicken into bite-sized small pieces & line your ingredients up (Chicken, cheese, mushrooms & bacon).
8. Heat a frying pan over medium heat & spread a small amount of butter on the bottom.
9. Prepare the tortillas by spreading a small amount of butter on the outsides.
10. Place a tortilla, butter side down & add in the chicken, mushrooms, bacon & lastly the cheese (ensure that you don't overfill). Place the other tortilla, butter side up on top. Once the bottom side of the tortilla turns golden; carefully flip & do the same with the other side as well.
11. Repeat these steps until you have used the ingredients completely.
12. Use the leftover honey mustard for dipping. Serve and enjoy.

Outback Steakhouse Blooming Onion

Prep Time: 10 minutes
Cooking Time: 10 minutes
Servings: 4 persons

Ingredients

- 2 tablespoons mayonnaise
- ½ teaspoon thyme, dried
- 2 tablespoons sour cream
- 1 ½ teaspoons ketchup
- 2 tablespoons paprika
- 1 tablespoon horseradish, drained
- ¼ teaspoon paprika
- 1 pound sweet onion, large-sized
- ½ teaspoon Worcestershire sauce
- 1 teaspoon cayenne pepper
- 2 ½ cups flour, all-purpose
- ½ teaspoon ground cumin
- 1 cup whole milk
- 2 large eggs
- ½ teaspoon oregano, dried
- 1 gallon corn or soy oil
- Freshly ground black pepper, kosher salt & cayenne pepper, to taste

Directions

1. Combine mayonnaise together with paprika, ketchup, sour cream, Worcestershire sauce, cayenne pepper, horseradish, black pepper and kosher salt in a large bowl. Using a plastic wrap; cover the bowl & place it in a refrigerator until ready to use.
2. Slice the onion; cutting it off ½" from the pointy stem end of the onion and then peel.
3. Placing the onion cut-side down, start ½" from the root & make a downward cut all the way through to the cutting board.
4. Make four evenly spaced cuts around the onion by repeating each step.
5. Now, make 16 evenly spaced cuts by continuing slicing the onion between each section.
6. Turn the onion over & gently separate the outer pieces using your fingers.
7. Combine flour with paprika, cayenne, oregano, thyme, cumin & ½ teaspoon of the black pepper in a separate bowl; with a whisk.
8. Whisk eggs, 1 cup water and milk in a small-sized bowl.
9. After placing the onion in a separate bowl with the cut-side up, pour the flour mixture completely over the top.
10. Cover the bowl with a large plate; shaking back & forth to distribute the flour; ensure that the onion is completely coated, especially among the flower petals from the cutting.
11. Lifting the onion by the core, turn over & pat off any excess flour; reserving the bowl with the flour.
12. Now, using a large slotted spoon; submerge the onion completely into the egg mixture.
13. Remove the onion, letting the excess egg to drip off & then repeat the flouring process.
14. Place the onion in a refrigerator and heat your oil over medium-high heat in a large deep pot until a deep-fry thermometer reflects 400 F.
15. Pat any excess flour off of the onion.
16. Lower the onion, cut-side down carefully into the oil using a wire skimmer; feel free to adjust the heat of the oil, ensure it's not over 350 F.
17. Cook the onion for 3 to 4 minutes per side, until turn golden.
18. Place them on paper towels to drain.
19. Salt to taste & serve with the dip. Enjoy.

Outback Steakhouse Kookaburra Wings

Prep Time: 20 minutes
Cooking Time: 20 minutes
Servings: 10 persons

Ingredients

- 48 ounces shortening
- 10 chicken wing drumettes

For Wing Coating:
- ¾ teaspoon freshly-ground black pepper
- 2 tablespoon all-purpose flour
- ¼ teaspoon garlic powder
- 1 teaspoon chili powder
- ½ teaspoon cayenne pepper
- ¼ teaspoon paprika
- 1 tablespoon Kraft Macaroni & Cheese cheddar cheese topping
- ¼ teaspoon onion powder
- 1 dash ground clove
- 1/8 teaspoon ground cumin
- 1 ¼ teaspoon salt

For the Sauce:
- 2 tablespoon Crystal Louisiana hot sauce
- 1 teaspoon water

For on the side:
- Celery sticks
- Bleu cheese dressing

Directions

1. Preheat 6 to 10 cups of vegetable oil or a large can of shortening to 350 F in advance.
2. Prepare the spiced breading by combining wing coating ingredients in a medium-sized bowl; give them a good stir. Slowly dip each wing into the breading; giving each wings a light coating of the mixture.
3. Place the breaded wings on a large plate & let sit in a refrigerator for 15 minutes, uncovered.
4. When the oil is hot; carefully add & fry the wings until the wings turn brown and are cooked through, for 7 to 10 minutes.
5. In the meantime, mix the hot sauce with water in a small bowl. When you have fried the wings, place them on a rack or paper towels to drain. Drop the hot wings into a large plastic container with a lid. Pour the prepared sauce on top of the wings. Cover & shake until the wings are nicely coated with the sauce.
6. Remove the wings from the container using a pair of tongs. Arrange them on a plate with the celery sticks and bleu cheese dressing on the side. Serve and enjoy.

Romano's Macaroni Grill Crispy Brussels Sprouts

Prep Time: 15 minutes
Cooking Time: 30 minutes
Servings: 6

Ingredients

- 2 pounds Brussels sprouts, fresh, trimmed & halved
- ⅓ cup dried cranberries
- 2 ounces sliced pancetta or bacon strips, chopped
- ½ cup pine nuts, toasted
- 2 garlic cloves, minced
- 1 tablespoon balsamic vinegar
- 3 tablespoons olive oil, divided
- ¼ teaspoon pepper
- ½ teaspoon salt

Directions

1. Preheat your oven to 400 F in advance. Place the Brussels sprouts in a 15x10x1" baking pan; toss with 2 tablespoons of oil, pepper and salt. Roast in the preheated oven until lightly charred & tender, for 30-35 minutes, stirring halfway.
2. In the meantime, heat the leftover oil over moderate heat in a large skillet until hot. Once done; add in the pancetta & cook until crisp or for 4 to 6 minutes, stirring frequently. Add in the garlic & cook for a minute more. Remove from heat and then stir in the vinegar.
3. Combine the Brussels sprouts together with pancetta mixture and cranberries in a large bowl; toss well. Sprinkle pine nuts on top. Serve and enjoy.

Outback Steakhouse Gold Coast Coconut Shrimp

Prep Time: 25 minutes
Cooking Time: 15 minutes
Servings: 4

Ingredients

- ¼ cup grey poupon country mustard
- 12 jumbo shrimp; peeled, deveined, washed & drained
- ½ teaspoon cayenne pepper
- 2 cups coconut, short shredded
- ½ cup orange marmalade
- 1 cup Ice water
- ½ cup cornstarch
- 3-4 drop of Tabasco sauce
- ½ cup flour
- 2 tablespoon vegetable oil
- ¼ cup honey
- 1 teaspoon salt
- ½ teaspoon cayenne pepper

Directions

1. Combine the entire dry ingredients for the batter together in a large bowl. Add 2 tablespoon of oil & ice water; give them a good stir until blended well.
2. Now, over moderate heat in a deep fryer; heat the oil to 350 F.
3. Spread coconut on a flat pan a small quantity at a time, adding more as required.
4. Dip the shrimp into the prepared batter and then roll it into the coconut. Fry for 3 to 4 minutes, until turn lightly browned.
5. Serve with Creole Marmalade and enjoy.

For Creole Marmalade:
1. Combine Grey Poupon mustard together with marmalade, honey, Tabasco sauce & cayenne pepper to taste.

Olive Garden Buschetta

Prep Time: 1 hour & 5 minutes
Cooking Time: 15 minutes
Servings: 8 persons

Ingredients

- 1½ pounds Ripe plum tomatoes (8 to 9 medium size), seeded & chopped roughly into ¼" pieces
- 1 garlic clove, minced
- 24 ½" slices of French or Italian bread
- 1-2 tablespoon balsamic vinegar, to taste
- 2 tablespoon fresh Italian flat-leaf parsley, minced
- 1 tablespoon fresh sweet Italian basil, minced
- 4-5 garlic cloves, large, whole & peeled
- ¼-cup extra-virgin olive oil
- 1 teaspoon sea or kosher salt
- Freshly ground black pepper, to taste

Directions

1. Place the chopped tomatoes into a colander & toss them with salt; let drain for an hour.
2. In the meantime; preheat your oven to 375 F in advance.
3. Combine drained tomatoes together with the basil, garlic & parsley in a medium bowl. Slowly mix in the balsamic vinegar and olive oil until blended well. Season with black pepper and salt to taste; set aside.
4. Place the bread on a baking sheet & toast in the preheated oven until crisp & golden, for 5 minutes. When done; rub the garlic cloves over the toasted surfaces.
5. Arrange the toasted bread on a large-sized serving platter & place approximately a tablespoon of the tomato mixture on each. Serve immediately and enjoy.

Olive Garden Stuffed Mushrooms

Prep Time: 20 minutes
Cooking Time: 45 minutes
Servings: 4

Ingredients

- 8 to 12 mushrooms, cleaned & stems removed
- 1 can clams, (6 oz) drained & finely minced; reserving approximately ¼ cup of the juice
- ¼ cup plus 2 tablespoon mozzarella cheese, finely grated
- 1 green onion, minced finely
- ½ teaspoon garlic, minced
- 1 teaspoon dried oregano
- ½ cup Italian bread crumbs, dried
- 1 tablespoon Romano cheese, finely grated
- 2 tablespoon parmesan cheese, finely grated
- 1 tablespoon butter, melted & slightly cooled
- ¼ cup butter, melted
- 1 beaten egg, large
- 1/8 teaspoon garlic salt

Directions

1. Lightly grease a small-sized baking dish & preheat your oven to 350 F in advance.
2. Combine clams together with minced garlic, garlic salt, green onion, oregano and 1 tablespoon butter in a large bowl. Add in the egg, bread crumbs & clam juice; mix well. Stir in the Romano, parmesan & 2 tablespoons of the mozzarella cheese. Place 1 ½ teaspoons of the prepared clam stuffing mixture inside each mushroom cavity & slightly mound. Place the stuffed mushrooms in the baking dish & pour ¼ cup of the melted butter on top.
3. Cover & bake in the preheated oven for 35 to 40 minutes. Uncover & sprinkle ¼ cup of the mozzarella cheese over the top; bake again until the cheese just melts.

Olive Garden Toasted Ravioli

Prep Time: 15 minutes
Cooking Time: 55 minutes
Servings: 6 persons

Ingredients

- 1 package Meat Ravioli, thawed (16 oz)
- 1 cup breadcrumbs
- 2 large eggs
- 1 teaspoon Basil
- ½ teaspoon oregano
- 1 cup flour
- ¼ cup water
- 1 teaspoon garlic salt

For Garnish:
- Grated parmesan

Directions

1. Beat eggs together with water in a large bowl.
2. Combine bread crumbs together with basil, oregano and garlic salt in a separate bowl.
3. Place flour into a third bowl.
4. Now, preheat your oil to 350 F in advance.
5. Dip each piece of ravioli first into the flour then into the egg wash & finally into the bread crumbs; set on plate for a couple of minutes.
6. Carefully place into the oil & fry for a couple of minutes, until turn golden.
7. Place on paper towels or a rack to drain.
8. Sprinkle with Parmesan; serve with marinara sauce on side & enjoy.

Olive Garden Mozzarella Fonduta

Prep Time: 5 minutes
Cooking Time: 15 minutes
Servings: 4

Ingredients

- 1 loaf Italian bread cut into slices or bite-sized pieces
- 8 ounces smoked mozzarella cheese, shredded
- 1 cup sour cream
- 8 ounces provolone cheese, shredded
- 1 tablespoon fresh parsley, chopped
- ½ cup parmesan cheese, finely grated
- 1 roma tomato, diced
- A pinch of red pepper flake
- 1 teaspoon Italian seasoning

Directions

1. Preheat your oven to 450 F in advance.
2. Combine provolone cheese together with the sour cream, parmesan cheese, mozzarella cheese, red pepper flake and Italian seasoning in a large bowl.
3. Lightly coat a 1.5 quarts casserole dish with the non-stick spray
4. Pour the prepared mixture into the dish.
5. Bake in the preheated oven until the mixture is melted and bubbly, for 12 to 15 minutes. Garnish with parsley and diced tomatoes.
6. Bake the bread slices for a couple of minutes and then serve immediately. Enjoy.

Sonic Extreme Tots

Prep Time: 5 minutes
Cooking Time: 35 minutes
Servings: 2

Ingredients

- ¼ cup white onions, diced
- ½ cup cheddar cheese, shredded
- 2 cups tater tots, frozen
- ¼ cup pickled jalapeños
- ½ cup chili
- ¼ cup ranch dressing

Directions

1. Cook the frozen tater tots as per the directions provided by the manufacturer.
2. Place the tater tots into a paper boat or bowl; cover with the cheddar cheese and chili. Microwave until the cheese is completely melted, for 45 seconds, on high-power. Top with the pickled jalapeños, white onions & a drizzle of the ranch dressing. Serve warm and enjoy.

Simon Kitchen & Bar Wok-Charred Edamame

Prep Time: 20 minutes
Cooking Time: 40 minutes
Servings: 4

Ingredients

- ½ pound frozen edamame, thawed
- 1 teaspoon Szechwan seasoning salt
- Juice of 1 lime, freshly squeezed
- 1 tablespoon light olive oil

Directions

1. Preheat a cast iron or wok over medium high heat until hot.
2. Now, in a small bowl; toss the edamame with the olive oil until coated well; remove & carefully drop them into the hot pan using your hands. Cook until the pods are blackened in spots, for 4 to 5 minutes, stirring frequently.
3. Remove the beans from the pan using a pair of tongs and drop them into a clean bowl. Pour the freshly squeezed lime juice on top; toss well. Add seasonings to taste; toss again. Serve immediately & enjoy.

Taco Bell Mexican Pizza

Prep Time: 10 minutes
Cooking Time: 25 minutes
Servings: 4

Ingredients

- ½ cup canned tomatoes, diced, drained
- 2 tortillas (8" each)
- ½ cup refried beans
- 1 green onion, sliced
- ⅓ cup Mexican blend cheese, shredded
- ¼ cup taco sauce

Directions

1. Lightly coat a large skillet with the cooking spray and preheat your oven to 400 F in advance.
2. Heat the tortillas for a minute or two on each side and then heat the refried beans.
3. Spread the refried beans entirely over one of the tortillas.
4. Place the leftover tortilla on top.
5. Place the combined tortillas on a large-sized baking sheet.
6. Spread the taco sauce on top of the tortilla.
7. Add in the onions, tomatoes and shredded cheese.
8. Bake in the preheated oven until the cheese is just melted, for 8 to 10 minutes. Serve immediately & enjoy.

Taco Bell Crunch Wrap Supreme

Prep Time: 20 minutes
Cooking Time: 25 minutes
Servings: 4

Ingredients

- 1 cup cheddar, shredded
- 8 large flour tortillas
- 1 pound ground beef
- ½ teaspoon ground paprika
- 1 teaspoon chili powder
- ½ teaspoon ground cumin
- 1 cup sour cream
- ½ cup nacho cheese sauce
- 1 cup Monterey Jack, shredded
- 4 tostada shells
- 1 cup chopped tomatoes
- 2 cup lettuce, shredded
- 1 tablespoon vegetable oil
- Freshly ground black pepper & kosher salt to taste

Directions

1. Over medium heat in a large nonstick skillet; combine ground beef together with the spices and then season with pepper and salt. Cook for 5 to 6 minutes, until no longer pink, breaking up meat using a large-sized wooden spoon. Drain the fat & wipe the skillet clean.
2. Stack 4 flour tortillas & place tostada shell in middle. Trace around the edges of shell to cut 4 smaller flour tortilla rounds using a paring knife.
3. For Crunch Wraps: Add a scoop of the ground beef to the middle of leftover flour tortillas, leaving a generous border for folding. Drizzle the cheese sauce on each and then place a tostada shell over the top. Spread the sour cream on each shell and then top with the lettuce, cheeses and tomato. Place the smaller flour tortilla cutouts on top & tightly fold the edges of large tortilla toward the middle, creating pleats. Quickly invert the Crunch Wraps.
4. Now, over medium heat in the same skillet; heat the oil until hot. Add in the Crunch Wrap & cook for 3 minutes per side, until tortilla is golden, seam-side down. Repeat with the leftover Crunch Wraps.

Texas Roadhouse Fried Pickles

Prep Time: 10 minutes
Cooking Time: 10 minutes
Servings: 4

Ingredients

For the Pickles:
- 1/8 teaspoon cayenne pepper
- 2 cups dill pickles, drained and sliced
- ¼ cup flour
- 1 teaspoon Cajun seasoning
- ¼ teaspoon basil
- Vegetable oil
- ¼ teaspoon oregano
- Kosher salt to taste

For the Dip:
- 1 tablespoon ketchup
- ¼ teaspoon Cajun seasoning
- 1 tablespoon horseradish
- ¼ cup mayonnaise

Directions

1. Over moderate heat in a large saucepan; heat the oil until hot.
2. Combine the entire dipping ingredients together in a small bowl; set aside until ready to use.
3. Place approximately 1 ½" of the vegetable oil in a wide pot & heat it over medium high heat.
4. Combine flour together with basil, oregano, Cajun seasoning, pepper & salt in a medium-sized bowl.
5. Work in batches and fry the pickles; ensure that you don't over-crowd them.
6. Coat the pickles with the flour mixture; shaking off any excess. Gently add the pickles to the hot oil.
7. Fry until the pickles turn golden brown, for 2 to 3 minutes. Using a large-sized slotted spoon; remove the pickles & place them on paper towel to drain.
8. Serve immediately with the dipping sauce and enjoy.

Texas Roadhouse Rattlesnake Bites

Prep Time: 40 minutes
Cooking Time: 10 minutes
Servings: 18

Ingredients

- 1 large egg
- 2 blocks Pepper Jack cheese, shredded (8 ounces each)
- 1 teaspoon garlic powder
- ½ cup flour
- 1 teaspoon paprika
- 2-3 diced jalapenos
- 1 teaspoon cayenne pepper
- 1 ½ cup bread crumbs
- 1 cup milk
- Oil for frying

Directions

1. Combine the shredded cheese with jalapenos in a large bowl.
2. Make approximately 1 ½" balls from the cheese mixture; squeezing the balls tightly to compress. Arrange them on a cookie sheet & freeze for half an hour.
3. In the meantime; preheat your deep fryer to 350 F in advance. Now, add flour into the cheese mixture. Mix egg with milk in a separate bowl. Lastly stir the bread crumbs with seasonings in a separate bowl.
4. Roll the formed balls first into the flour mixture, then dip them into the milk & lastly coat them with the bread crumbs. Work in batches and fry the coated balls until turn golden brown, for 3 to 4 minutes.
5. Place them on paper towel to drain. Serve with your favorite dipping sauces and enjoy.

TGI Friday's Potato Skins

Prep Time: 25 minutes
Cooking Time: 55 minutes
Servings: 6

Ingredients

- 6 slices bacon, cooked & chopped
- 3 tablespoons butter, melted
- 1 cup sour cream
- 3 cups cheddar cheese, shredded
- 4-6 Russet Potatoes, small to medium sized
- ¼ cup green onions, chopped
- 2 tablespoons olive oil
- 1 teaspoon salt

Directions

1. Preheat your oven to 400 F in advance. Rub the potatoes with oil and arrange them on a large-sized baking sheet; using a sharp knife; pierce each a couple of times. Bake in the preheated oven until fork tender, for 35 to 40 minutes
2. Set aside and let cool until easy to handle then, slice in half lengthwise; scoop out the middle with a spoon; leaving approximately ½" of the walls intact. Place them, scoop side up to the baking sheet again.
3. Sprinkle the inside of the potatoes with salt & brush with the melted butter. Fill them with bacon and cheese. Place to the oven again & bake for 6 to 8 minutes, until the cheese has melted.
4. Top with green onions and sour cream; serve immediately & enjoy.

TGI Friday's Pretzel Sticks and Beer Cheese Dip

Prep Time: 10 minutes
Cooking Time: 30 minutes
Servings: 6

Ingredients

For Pretzel Sticks:
- 2 tablespoons plus 1 teaspoon sugar, divided
- 1 cup plus 2 tablespoons warm water
- 4 ½ to 5 cups all-purpose flour, plus more for rolling
- 1 egg white beaten lightly with 1 teaspoon of water, for glaze
- 8 cups for water
- ¼ cup baking soda
- 2 ½ teaspoons instant yeast
- 1 tablespoon course kosher salt, for sprinkling
- Vegetable oil for bowl
- 1 teaspoon salt

For Beer Cheese Sauce:
- 4 to 6 ounces beer
- 8 ounces American cheese; chopped into 1" cubes

Directions

For the Pretzel Sticks:
1. In a small bowl; combine the yeast with 1 teaspoon sugar & 2 tablespoons of warm water. The yeast is ready to use once it starts to foam & bubble. Transfer the yeast mixture to the bowl of a stand mixer & then add the flour and salt; start mixing the ingredients using the dough hook. Slowly stream the leftover warm water into the flour and continue to mix until a ball of dough forms. Continue mixing for a minute more.
2. Lightly grease the bowl with vegetable oil and then place the dough ball in middle of your coated bowl. Using kitchen towel; cover the bowl and let rise until almost double in size, for 35 minutes.
3. Four a cutting board & place the dough on the board. Knead & then evenly divide the dough into 16 portions. Roll each portion into a cigar shape & cut 2 or 3 slits into the top using a sharp knife. Cover with a towel & let rise for 25 more minutes.
4. Preheat your oven to 375 F in advance.
5. Now, over moderate heat in a large saucepan; heat 8 cups of water until starts boiling. Immediately add the baking soda & leftover sugar. Work in batches and drop pretzel sticks into the boiling water (4 pretzel sticks at a time); cook for 30 seconds per side. Remove the sticks using a slotted spoon & place them on a large-sized baking sheet.
6. Brush the pretzels with the egg white glaze & generously sprinkle with the coarse salt. Bake in the preheated oven for 20 to 25 minutes, until brown. Transfer to a wire rack & let cool for 8 to 10 minutes. Serve warm and enjoy.

For the Cheese Sauce:
1. Place the cheese cubes with 4 ounces of beer in a small saucepan. Heat until the cheese is completely melted, over low heat, stirring frequently.

TGI Friday's Crispy Green Bean Fries

Prep Time: 45 minutes
Cooking Time: 1 hour & 15 minutes
Servings: 4

Ingredients

For the Beans:
- 2 cup low-salt chicken broth
- ½ cup milk
- 1 large egg
- ¼ teaspoon onion powder
- 1 cup instant flour
- A pinch of cayenne pepper
- ½ pound green beans, trimmed
- 1 cup breadcrumbs
- Vegetable or peanut oil, for frying
- 1/8 teaspoon garlic powder
- Black pepper & kosher salt to taste

For the Dip:
- 2 teaspoon wasabi powder
- 1 tablespoon horseradish, drained
- ½ cup cucumber, peeled, chopped & seeded
- 1 tablespoon milk
- ½ cup ranch dressing
- A pinch cayenne pepper
- 1 teaspoon distilled white vinegar
- Kosher salt

Directions

1. For the Dip: Puree the cucumber together with vinegar, dressing, milk, horseradish, cayenne pepper, wasabi powder & salt to taste in a blender until completely smooth. Cover & refrigerate until ready to use.
2. For the Beans: Fill a large bowl with ice water. Over moderate heat in a large saucepan; bring broth to a boil. Add the green beans & cook for 5 to 6 minutes, until tender. Using a large-sized slotted spoon; remove the beans & transfer them to the ice water. Let cool in the water, then drain & pat them dry.
3. Whisk the milk and egg in a large-sized shallow bowl. Put ½ cup of the flour in a separate shallow bowl. Combine breadcrumbs together with the leftover flour, garlic powder, onion powder, cayenne, pepper & salt to taste in a separate bowl.
4. Line a large-sized baking sheet with the parchment paper. Toss the green beans into the flour; shaking off any excess then, dip into the egg mixture and then dredge into the breadcrumb mixture. Arrange them on the baking sheet. Freeze for 30 minutes, until the coating is set.
5. Over medium heat in a deep pot; heat 3" oil until hot and fry green beans for 1 to 2 minutes, until golden brown, in batches. Transfer the beans with a skimmer or tongs to paper towels or a rack to drain. Serve with the dip and enjoy.

TGI Fridays' BBQ Chicken Wings

Prep Time: 1 hour & 15 minutes
Cooking Time: 15 minutes
Servings: 5

Ingredients

- ½ cup flour
- ¼ cup hot sauce
- 10 chicken wings
- ¼ cup margarine
- ½ teaspoon paprika
- ⅛ teaspoon each of garlic powder & fresh ground black pepper
- ¼ teaspoon each of cayenne pepper & kosher salt

Directions

1. Combine flour together with cayenne pepper, paprika & salt in a small-sized mixing bowl. Toss the chicken wings in the seasoning mixture. Cover & let refrigerate for an hour.
2. Preheat your deep fryer to 375 F in advance.
3. Combine margarine together with hot sauce, garlic powder and ground pepper in a small saucepan. Cook until the sauce is heated through & margarine has melted, over low heat. Immediately remove from the heat & set aside.
4. Add wings to the preheated deep fryer & fry until wings start to turn brown, for 12 to 15 minutes. Toss the wings in hot sauce; serve immediately & enjoy.

Get Free Recipe eBooks!
Cookbook Club

Fabulous Free eBook Cookbooks Every Week!

Our eBooks are FREE for the first few days publication. Be the first to know when new books are published. Our collection includes hundreds of books on topics including healthy foods, diets, food allergy alternatives, gourmet meals, desserts, and easy and inexpensive meals.

Join the mailing list at:
EncoreBookClub.com

Related Copycat Books
Copycat Candy Recipes
http://url80.com/copycatcandy
Homemade Copycat Liqueurs
http://url80.com/copycatliqueur
Copycat Olive Garden Recipes
http://url80.com/copycatolive
Copycat PF Chang's Recipes
http://url80.com/copycatpfchang
Copycat Dessert Recipes
http://url80.com/copycatdessert
Copycat Applebee's Recipes
http://url80.com/copycatapplebee
Copycat Panera Bread Recipes
http://url80.com/copycatpanera
Copycat TGI Friday's Recipes
http://url80.com/fridays

Thank You for Your Purchase!

We know you have many choices when it comes to ready and recipe books. Your patronage is sincerely appreciated. If you would like to provide us feedback, go to http://url8o.com/feedback.

Please Consider Writing an Amazon Review!

Happy with this book? If so, please consider writing a positive review. It helps others know it's a quality book and allows us to continue to promote our positive message. To write reviews, go to http://url8o.com/reviews.

Thank You!

Made in the USA
Coppell, TX
28 March 2020